FOREIGN AFFAIRS

Special Collection

Foreign Affairs Special Collection: The ISIS Crisis

Editor Gideon Rose Introduces the Collection

With the Islamic State of Iraq and al-Sham still on the rampage and at the top of the U.S. national security agenda, we at *Foreign Affairs* have put together a follow-up to our earlier eBook, *Endgame in Iraq*. In this collection, our authors examine the nature of the ISIS threat, the current state of the war against it, and the options for what to do next. We can't promise that after reading it, you'll know exactly what to do. But we can promise that you'll have the information you need to think about the question intelligently.

ON THE CHALLENGE
William McCants, a fellow at the Brookings Institution, explains that the idea of an Islamic state has a fatal flaw: its physical incarnation makes it vulnerable to attack.

ON STRATEGY
Audrey Kurth Cronin, a professor at George Mason University, argues that Washington's counterterrorism strategy will not work against ISIS, since ISIS is technically not a terrorist group.

ON THE FRONTS
Jytte Klausen, a professor at Brandeis University, measures the threat returning jihadists pose to the West.

ON THE RESPONSE
Foreign Affairs' brain trust weighs in on whether the United States should significantly step up its military campaign against ISIS in Iraq and Syria.

Visit ForeignAffairs.com for more on these topics—and all our other great content.

The New New Jihadist Thing

Meeting the ISIS Challenge

Gideon Rose

One of the signature beliefs of the George W. Bush administration was that Iraq was a crucial font of radical Sunni jihadism and so had to be attacked as an essential early move in the post-9/11 "war on terror." At the time, this proposition was dubious. Iraqi leader Saddam Hussein's links to terror were real but relatively minor ones. As one wag put it, Iraq was low on the list of state sponsors of terror, and terrorism was low on the list of reasons to worry about Saddam's Iraq. (What professionals considered a much greater worry—Saddam's covert WMD programs—also turned out to be minor, but that's a story for another day.)

By toppling the Saddam regime and failing to put anything substantial in its place, however, the Bush administration created the conditions for its fears to be realized, and within a few years radical jihadists were crucial players in the chaos of Iraq's burgeoning civil war. Order was eventually restored through a combination of local tribal resistance, aggressive U.S. counterterrorism policies, and Washington's adoption of a new and better-resourced counterinsurgency strategy, and so by the time the last U.S. combat troops left Iraq at the end of 2011, radical Islamist terrorism was once again low on the list of the country's troubles.

GIDEON ROSE is Editor of *Foreign Affairs*.

Then three new factors came into play: increasingly inept and sectarian rule by the Shiite-led government, increasing detachment on the part of Washington, and increasing violence in neighboring Syria. Together, these kindled the glowing embers of the left-for-dead Iraqi jihadist movement. Elements of the group formerly known as al Qaeda in Iraq resurfaced as the Islamic State of Iraq and al-Sham, or ISIS; gained a foothold in the badlands of eastern Syria; and eventually conquered large swaths of western Iraq to boot, bringing death, destruction, and fanaticism in their wake.

We told this sorry story last summer, in our eBook *Endgame in Iraq*. Nine months later, with ISIS still on the rampage and at the top of the U.S. national security agenda, we think it's time to revisit the subject, carefully examining the nature of the ISIS threat, the current state of the war against it, and the options for what to do next.

Bringing together a collection of our best coverage of the subject from both print and Web, *The ISIS Crisis* offers an unparalleled range of authoritative analysis on everything from the group's ideology, strategy, and internal characteristics; to its operations across the Middle East and elsewhere; to the difficult tradeoffs involved in trying to halt and reverse its advance.

As you'd expect from *Foreign Affairs,* we don't waste our time with juvenilia, such as whether jihadists are crossing the Rio Grande or debating whether the word "Islamic" should figure prominently in White House rhetoric. Instead, we look at the real questions worthy of debate: What does ISIS want? How great a threat does it pose, to whom? And how can it be stopped? The collection concludes with a fascinating survey of expert opinion on whether Washington should step up its anti-ISIS military campaign, in which 73 of the world's most knowledgeable observers offer their personal take on the question.

We can't promise that after reading all this, you'll know exactly what to do. But we can promise that you'll have the information you need to think about the question intelligently.

The Myth of the Caliphate

The Political History of an Idea

Nick Danforth

In 1924, Turkish leader Kemal Ataturk officially abolished the Ottoman caliphate. Today, most Western discussions of the Islamic State of Iraq and al-Sham (ISIS), the extremist group that has declared a caliphate across much of Iraq and Syria, begin by referencing this event as if it were a profound turning point in Islamic history. Some contemporary Islamists think of it this way, too: there's a reason, for example, that *Lion Cub*, the Muslim Brotherhood's children's publication, once awarded the "Jewish" "traitor" Ataturk multiple first prizes in its "Know the Enemies of Your Religion" contest.

Even if today's Islamists reference the Ottomans, though, most of them are much more focused on trying to re-create earlier caliphates: the era of the four Rightly Guided Caliphs, who ruled immediately after Muhammad's death in the seventh century, for example, or the Abbasid caliphate, which existed in one form or another from the ninth to the thirteenth centuries (before being officially abolished by the Mongols). By conflating the nineteenth-century Ottoman royal family with these caliphs from a millennium ago or more, Western pundits and nostalgic Muslim thinkers alike have built up a narrative of the caliphate as an enduring

NICK DANFORTH is a doctoral candidate in Turkish history at Georgetown University.

institution, central to Islam and Islamic thought between the seventh and twentieth centuries. In fact, the caliphate is a political or religious idea whose relevance has waxed and waned according to circumstance.

The caliphate's more recent history under the Ottomans shows why the institution might be better thought of as a political fantasy—a blank slate just as nebulous as the "dictatorship of the proletariat"—that contemporary Islamists are largely making up as they go along. (If it weren't, ISIS could not so readily use the same term to describe their rogue and bloody statelet that Muslim British businessmen use to articulate the idea of an elected and democratic leader for the Islamic world.) What's more, the story of the Ottoman caliphate also suggests that in trying to realize almost any version of this fantasy, contemporary Islamists may well confront the same contradictions that bedeviled the Ottomans a century ago.

OTTOMAN REBRANDING

When the Ottoman Empire conquered Egypt and the Arabian Peninsula in 1517, Sultan Selim the Grim officially claimed the title of caliph for himself and his heirs. In addition to taking control of the cities of Mecca and Medina, Selim bolstered his claim by bringing a collection of the Prophet's garments and beard hairs back to Istanbul.

Centuries after the fact, the Ottomans decided that they needed to make the whole process look a little more respectable, so royal historians began to assert that the final heir to the Abbasid caliphate, living in exile in Cairo centuries after losing his throne, had voluntarily bestowed his title on Selim. More practically, the Ottomans buttressed their claim to Islamic leadership by serving as guardians of the hajj and sending an elaborately decorated gilt mantle to cover the Kaaba each year.

To put the title grab in perspective, when the Ottoman Sultan Mehmed II conquered the Byzantine capital of Constantinople 64 years before Selim conquered Egypt, he had claimed the title

Caesar of Rome for his descendants. To the extent that being caliph had any more purchase than being Caesar for the Ottomans in the late nineteenth century, it was largely the result of a political campaign on the part of Sultan Abdulhamid II to rally anticolonial sentiment around the Ottoman state and to boost his own domestic legitimacy. His techniques included seeking to have his name read out at Friday prayers and distributing Korans around the Muslim world from Africa to Indonesia.

There is no doubt that many Muslims, faced with the triumph of European colonialism in their own countries, did come to admire the idea of a pious and powerful leader like the Ottoman sultan defying Western imperialism on behalf of the entire Muslim world. Certainly, British and French officials expressed increasing fear about his potential power over Muslim colonial subjects in North Africa and India. Although he was eager to try to leverage such fears, however, even Abdulhamid had his misgivings about how much real influence his efforts won him in such far-flung locales.

One thing that particularly worried him was the fact that not everyone accepted his claims on the caliphate. Separate from those who rallied around Abdulhamid out of religious solidarity were others, motived by Arab nationalism or dissatisfaction with Abdulhamid's tyranny, who questioned the religious foundation of his rule. Such thinkers, including at some points Rashid Rida, justified the creation of a different, Arab caliphate by quoting Muhammad as saying that the true caliph needed to be a descendant of the Prophet's Quraysh tribe. (The Ottomans, it seems, accepted the validity of this quote but had their own interpretation of it, in which the Prophet actually meant that the caliph didn't need to be a descendant of the Quraysh tribe.)

But in either case, the violent politics of the early twentieth century quickly outmatched theology. Despite his best efforts as defender of the faith, Abdulhamid kept losing territory and political power to Christian imperialist forces. That helped the secular leaders of the Young Turk movement, such as Enver Pasha, sideline the sultan and take power for themselves on the eve of World War I. When the Ottoman Empire then enjoyed some military success, belatedly holding its own in the Second Balkan War, Enver became an inspiration to the Muslim world. Indeed, the list of babies reportedly named after him at the time includes Enver Hoxha, the future leader of Albania, and Anwar al-Sadat, the future leader of Egypt.

ARAB HEIR

Of course, Enver's own star faded, too, with the Ottoman defeat at the end of World War I. Ataturk quickly emerged as a new hero by leading a successful campaign to drive French, Italian, British, and Greek armies out of Ottoman Anatolia. Quickly, some of the same politically attuned Muslims who had supported Abdulhamid's anti-imperial caliphate found even more to admire in Ataturk's armed defiance of European might. In Palestine, for example, Muslims who had once turned to the Ottoman caliph for protection against Zionist settlers and British occupiers began to cheer Ataturk, leading one suspicious British officer to worry that the Turkish figure had become "a new savior of Islam."

At the same time, the decline of Ottoman power before, during, and after World War I loaned increasing credence to the idea of a new, non-Ottoman caliph in the Arab world. But it was never entirely clear just who that Arab caliph would be. The result was that when Ataturk finally abolished the institution of the caliphate in 1924, there was no clear or coherent outcry from the Muslim world as a whole. Many Muslims, particularly those in India for whom pan-Islamic symbols such as the caliph were an important part of anticolonialism, protested. Others were more interested in maneuvering to claim the title for themselves.

Most famous was Husayn ibn Ali, sherif of Mecca, who is known to Lawrence of Arabia fans for his leading role in the Arab Revolt. As the local leader with control of Mecca and Medina—and a supposedly clear line of descent from the Prophet's tribe—Husayn believed that after driving the Ottomans out of the Middle East, he could become an Arab king, with all the religious and temporal powers of the caliph. In pursuit of this goal, when Ataturk exiled the Ottoman sultan, Husayn invited him to Mecca. (The exiled monarch soon decided he preferred the Italian Riviera.)

Several years later, Husayn's son Abdullah—founder of the Jordanian monarchy—would declare that, in ending the caliphate, Turks had "rendered the greatest possible service to the Arabs," for which he felt like "sending a telegram thanking Mustafa Kemal." Of course, Husayn's plans didn't come off exactly as expected. Despite getting British backing for his scheme early in the war, he famously fell afoul of the Sykes-Picot Agreement. The French drove his son out of Syria, and before long, the Saudis drove him out of the Arabian Peninsula. By the time Husayn officially declared himself caliph, supposedly at the insistence of a select group of Muslim leaders, his power had dwindled to the point where the declaration seemed like an act of pure desperation.

The Egyptian monarchy, meanwhile, had a claim of its own to advance. Despite being closely aligned with the British and descended from Circassian Albanian ancestors with no tie to the Prophet's family, King Fuad covertly put forward his case to succeed the Ottomans. In the words of one Islamic scholar, Egypt was better suited to the caliphate than, say, a desert nomad like Husayn "because she took the lead in religious education and had a vast number of highly educated and intelligent Muslims." King Idris I of Libya also seemed to consider making a bid for the title but, like Fuad, ultimately decided he had too little support to do so officially.

Saudi Arabia's King Saud, despite eventually seizing the Holy Land from Husayn, was one of the few leaders who never put forward a claim to the caliphate, although the idea was certainly discussed. Saud was aligned with the Wahhabi movement, which arose as a rebellion against the supposed decadence of the Ottoman government in the eighteenth century. Ironically, although his opposition to the Ottoman-style caliph was shared by other Arabs, his particular brand of religiosity was too radical for him to ever think he had much chance of becoming caliph himself.

In the end, though, the unseemliness of such political wrangling was just one of the factors that helped put the caliphate discussion to rest for the next several decades. Many Muslims had responded to its abolition by redoubling their efforts to build secular constitutional governments in their own countries. Indeed, some of the strongest opposition to the Egyptian king's caliphal aspirations came from Egyptian liberals who opposed any moves that would increase the monarchy's power. Egyptian scholar Ali Abd al-Raziq, in his famously controversial criticism of the very idea of a caliphate, even went so far as to claim that the Koran contains "no reference to the caliphate that Muslims have been calling for." This was also the period where a number of thinkers, secularists and religious Muslims alike, began discussing the possibility that the caliph should be a purely religious figure, like an "Islamic pope," unencumbered by any temporal power.

A HOPE AND A PRAYER

It would be a mistake to think that twenty-first-century Islamist movements trying to revive the caliphate are doing so in the name of a clear, well-defined Islamic mandate. Rather, they are just other players in a centuries-long debate about a concept that has only occasionally taken on widespread relevance in the Islamic world.

The legacy of earlier rounds of this argument can still be felt today. It is no surprise that, as a historical inspiration, the Ottoman caliphate holds most sway among Turkish Islamists, whose nostalgia owes far more to the way Turkish nationalists have glorified the empire than it does to the piety of the sultans. Conversely, the religious legacy of Abd al-Wahhab's eighteenth-century critique of the Ottoman state, combined with the political legacy of more recent anti-Ottoman Arab nationalism, gives plenty of non-Turkish Islamists ample reason to prefer the precedent of an Arab caliphate.

By treating the Ottoman caliphate as the final historical reference point for what current Islamists aspire to, Western pundits conflate the contemporary dream of a powerful, universally respected Muslim leader with the late Ottoman sultan's failed dream of becoming such a figure himself. The circumstances uniting these dreams—and the appeal of strong religious power in the face of Western political, military, and economic power—may be the same. But so are the challenges. Contemporary claimants to the title of caliph may quickly find themselves in the same boat as Ottoman caliphs. Political or military success, rather than history or theology, can bring short-lived legitimacy, but failure in these realms will bring other contenders for power.

Collateral Damage in Iraq

The Rise of ISIS and the Fall of al Qaeda

Barak Mendelsohn

O n its lightning-fast advance through Iraq, the radical jihadi group the Islamic State of Iraq and al-Sham (ISIS) has captured Mosul, Iraq's second-largest city; Tikrit, Saddam Hussein's birth city; and many other towns along the way. Now, with help from former Baathists and Sunni tribal forces, the group is making its way toward Baghdad. ISIS' astonishing success could be a harbinger of a tectonic shift within the jihadi movement. Namely, ISIS could supplant al Qaeda as the movement's leader.

This showdown has been several years in the making. The friction between the two groups goes back years. But the relationship did not reach a breaking point until April 2013, when Abu Bakr al-Baghdadi, the leader of ISIS, expanded his group into Syria and attempted to subordinate the local al Qaeda branch, Jabhat al-Nusra (JN), to his own authority. JN rejected Baghdadi's leadership, and Ayman al-Zawahiri, al Qaeda's chief, tried to calm the dispute by announcing that JN would remain responsible for jihad in the Syrian arena and ISIS would keep to Iraq. ISIS refused to accept Zawahiri's decision and continued its expansion into Syria.

BARAK MENDELSOHN is an Associate Professor of political science at Haverford College and a Senior Fellow at the Foreign Policy Research Institute (FPRI). Follow him on Twitter @BarakMendelsohn.

Along the way, it trampled other Syrian rebel groups, including radical Islamists. Soon, ISIS' overreach provoked a backlash, and opposing rebel groups mounted a counteroffensive. For its part, JN eventually sided with the anti-ISIS forces. By February 2014, the rift between ISIS and the Syrian opposition had led Zawahiri to disown the group.

The differences between ISIS, on the one side, and al Qaeda and JN, on the other, are not merely about power and control of the jihadi movement. As important as these aspects are, the groups have serious differences when it comes to strategy, tactics, and Islamic authority. They differ on issues such as the implementation of harsh Islamist laws, the killing of Shia civilians, and the right of one group to impose its authority over all others. The groups don't disagree about the legitimacy of all of these things, but al Qaeda is more patient and ISIS is generally more radical and uncompromising. For that reason, its traipse through Iraq represents a serious organizational, strategic, and ideological blow to al Qaeda.

ISIS' display of power will likely strengthen its hand over al Qaeda in Syria and beyond. First, the military successes brought the group substantial spoils: ISIS looted bank deposits worth close to $500 million, captured large quantities of military equipment, and liberated hundreds of fighters from prisons in territory now under its control. All of that will prove very useful in Iraq and in Syria. As money and manpower breed success, success will breed more success. ISIS' popularity will likely rise among radicals, and that will translate into more funding and volunteers for the group. ISIS could rapidly mobilize those forces along the vanishing border between Iraq and Syria, which it now increasingly controls, and launch even more ambitious campaigns while it fends off attacks in Syria.

Second, beyond raising ISIS' profile, the terrorist group's march through Iraq also diminishes al Qaeda's. Al Qaeda's greatest achievement was the 9/11 attacks, but that was 13 years ago. Many of today's jihadis were young children at that time. Moreover, the attack on the United States was only supposed to be a means to an end: the establishment of an Islamic caliphate in the heart of the

Middle East. Al Qaeda franchises did manage to gain (and then lose) some territory in Yemen, Somalia, and northern Mali. But these territories are smaller in size and significance than what al Qaeda wanted—and what ISIS controls today. Although al Qaeda may have started the march toward the reestablishment of the Caliphate, it is ISIS that seems to be realizing it.

Third, success breeds legitimacy. For the past year, al Qaeda's main tactic against ISIS has been to try to delegitimize the movement. And, until now, al Qaeda's strategy had been moderately successful. Popular jihadi scholars, such as Abu Muhammad al-Maqdisi and Abu Qatada al-Filistini, released messages of support for al Qaeda and strongly denounced ISIS—which turned some would-be adherents away from the upstart. ISIS was able to muddle through the delegitimization campaign by hanging on to the support of some young and popular jihadi scholars. And, even before the surprise in Iraq, the trend in the jihadi movement had been toward the decentralization of religious authority; social media offers a platform for nearly any charismatic jihadi to gain a following. At the same time, moreover, young jihadis have increasingly come to view the old guard—often identified with al Qaeda—as disconnected from reality. They give more respect to warriors than to religious scholars. All that plays to ISIS' favor, especially now that it has real victories under its belt. It can use those as evidence that it has been right all along and that its ways are truthful. Zawahiri's criticisms, delivered from his hiding place in Pakistan, are weak in comparison.

Fourth, symbolism works to ISIS' advantage. In the past, al Qaeda, Syrian rebel groups, and numerous jihadi scholars criticized Baghdadi's claim that ISIS represents a genuine Islamic Emirate—with rights that surpass any privileges a jihadi organization may claim—by arguing that control over territory is essential for the creation of Islamic Emirate. Now, ISIS holds territory larger than many countries. Similarly, although Baghdadi has been criticized for using the title Emir of the Believers, which is reserved for the Caliph, his organization's recent accomplishments make the title seem more appropriate. Further, it is lost on few radical Islamists that Baghdadi's forces—merely 5,000 men—defeated 90,000 soldiers on a march toward Baghdad, the seat of the Abbasid Caliphate for 500 years.

War is, of course, unpredictable, and ISIS' good omens could evaporate if it doesn't hold on to its gains. Unfortunately for al Qaeda (and Iraqis and Syrians), that seems unlikely to happen. ISIS' march is the result of a well-thought-out plan that was a long time in the making. The crumbling Iraqi military is ill equipped to quickly reverse ISIS' progress, and the United States appears unwilling to step in, at least in a dramatic way.

Al Qaeda knows that. And so, despite the animosity between the two groups, it seems to be bound to congratulate its rival for its victories. It might offer advice, but it can't go against ISIS. It will be expected to offer support or at the least cheer for its rival, not stick a knife in its back. To al Qaeda's further disadvantage, disagreements over methods and authority are increasingly less salient. Al Qaeda's appeal relative to ISIS' is greater when questions of how to run a territory populated by Sunni Muslims who do not subscribe to the Salafi-jihadi radical interpretation of Islam take center stage. When the front stabilizes and the intensity of the fight subsides, such questions will return and the inherent weakness of ISIS will resurface. ISIS is an extremely capable force, but its battle achievements do not make it any more appealing as a government. To succeed in the competition with ISIS, al Qaeda could try to outdo it in some way— through advances against the Assad regime, quality operations in the Arabian Peninsula and in North Africa, and attacks in the West. Still, given the weakening of al Qaeda's central command, the limitations of its franchises, and this most recent blow to its reputation, its ability to recover is far from certain.

State of Confusion

ISIS' Strategy and How to Counter It

William McCants

In 2005, Ayman al-Zawahiri, deputy head of al Qaeda, had a killer idea: the al Qaeda franchise in Iraq (AQI) should declare an Islamic state. In a letter to Abu Musab al-Zarqawi, the brutal leader of AQI, Zawahiri explained how it would work. The Islamic state, he wrote, would fill security vacuums around Iraq left by departing American forces. Once the Islamic state successfully fended off the attacks from neighboring countries that would undoubtedly follow, it could proclaim the reestablishment of the caliphate, the one-man institution that had ruled a vast empire in early Islamic history. For the scheme to succeed, Zawahiri warned Zarqawi, al Qaeda had to make sure that the Sunni masses supported the project.

Once it was loosed into the world, Zawahiri's idea was too powerful for him or the al Qaeda leadership to control. By 2006, long before the American withdrawal and far too early to have built up much popular backing, AQI had established Zawahiri's Islamic state. The new head of AQI after Zarqawi's death, Abu Ayyub al-Masri, dissolved his organization and pledged his allegiance to a new "commander of the faithful," Abu Omar al-Baghdadi, who purportedly controlled the Dawlat al Iraq al Islamiyya, or the Islamic State.

Baghdadi's title confused the jihadist community. In medieval Islam, "commander of the faithful" was usually reserved for the

WILLIAM MCCANTS is a Fellow in the Center for Middle East Policy and Director of the Project on U.S. Relations with the Islamic World at the Brookings Institution.

caliphs. Was Baghdadi claiming to be the caliph? And what of Mullah Omar, to whom al Qaeda's leaders had already pledged allegiance? The name of the group was also puzzling. The word for "state" in Arabic is *dawla*. Was the new group claiming to be a *dawla* in the modern sense, an institution jihadists believe is un-Islamic? Or was the Dawlat al Iraq al Islamiyya simply an ode to the great caliphate Dawla Abbasiyya?

The Islamic State was not eager to dispel the ambiguity. It either liked implying that it had more power than it actually possessed or believed that the jihadist community was not ready to tolerate the full freight of its claims. Ambiguous audacity captured the imagination and was thus the key to the group's power.

Although Zawahiri had first suggested the idea of establishing a state, he and the other al Qaeda leaders were blindsided by its early realization. Writing four years after the ISI was declared, Adam Gadahn, an American al Qaeda operative, confided in a private letter that "the decision to declare the State was taken without consultation from al'Qaida leadership," a move that "caused a split in the Mujahidin ranks and their supporters inside and outside Iraq."

Al Qaeda's official position, nevertheless, was to endorse the fait accompli, probably in an effort to keep a hand in the Iraq game and avoid further dissension in the ranks. "I want to clarify that there is nothing in Iraq by the name of al Qaeda," proclaimed Zawahiri in a December 2007 question-and-answer session. "Rather, the organization of [AQI] merged, by the grace of God, with other jihadi groups in the Islamic State of Iraq, may God protect it. It is a legitimate emirate established on a legitimate and sound method. It was established through consultation and won the oath of allegiance from most of the mujahids and tribes in Iraq." But neither point was true, as al Qaeda leaders privately groused.

Al Qaeda may have ratified its affiliate's decision to disband after the fact, but it was still an open question as to whether the Islamic State was subordinate to al Qaeda Central or an altogether independent entity. The state itself never addressed the question, again relying on ambiguity to imply greater power and independence than it actually possessed. And al Qaeda's leaders made the fateful decision never to dispel that uncertainty.

From private documents, though, we know that al Qaeda Central believed that the Islamic State was under its authority. In his private letter, for one, Gadahn claims as much. The United States also uncovered a paper trail of documents from 2007 and 2008 attesting to that fact. Al Qaeda Central ordered the Islamic State of Iraq to carry out attacks, for example, against Halliburton in 2007 and the Danes in 2008. Al Qaeda Central also asked for information on the state's personnel and expenditures. When the group refused to answer corruption charges leveled by one of its former officials, al Qaeda Central summoned Masri, the group's war minister and previously the head of AQI, to the woodshed in "Khorasan" (Afghanistan or Pakistan).

Whatever control al Qaeda exercised over the Islamic State of Iraq had further eroded by 2011, either because the Islamic State rarely heard from al Qaeda Central owing to U.S. counterterrorism measures or because the state did not want to listen to its superior. As Gadahn put it in his letter, "Operational relations between the leadership of al-Qaeda and the State have been cut off for quite some time."

Still, there was no formal break between the two organizations. Even Abu Muhammad al-Adnani, the Islamic State's spokesman, who today denies that the Islamic State of Iraq ever pledged an oath to obey al Qaeda, acknowledges that it was "loyal" to al Qaeda's commanders and addressed them as such, and that it continued to abide by al Qaeda's guidance on attacks outside Iraq. For example, he says, the group refrained from ever attacking Iran (even though its soldiers demanded it) out of deference to al Qaeda's desire to "protect its interests and its supply lines in Iran." The Islamic State also held back from carrying out attacks in Saudi Arabia, Egypt, Libya, and Tunisia because al Qaeda asked it to. But when it came to targeting decisions inside Iraq, the spokesman contends that it never followed al Qaeda's "repeated request" to stop targeting Shiites. And, in his telling, al Qaeda Central never issued a direct command or asked about the disposition of its forces inside Iraq. When al Qaeda's leaders expelled the group in 2014 for its disobedience, Adnani retorted that al Qaeda could not disown what had never belonged to it in the first place.

Adnani is lying, has a poor memory, or is unaware of high-level discussions between the Islamic State of Iraq and al Qaeda Central. Al Qaeda certainly inquired about the Islamic State's troops and issued requests and demands for it to change its targets, modify its tactics, and reform its bureaucracy, as the documents from 2007 and 2008 demonstrate. That al Qaeda usually couched its instructions in polite language does not mean al Qaeda expected the Islamic State to ignore them.

There are many reasons the Islamic State grew unruly, some of them bureaucratic—it is hard to govern a terrorist group remotely, especially when even the local leader loses control of a corrupt faction of the group—others security related—many of al Qaeda Central's messages were delayed or simply did not get through because of U.S. counterterrorism measures. But other al Qaeda affiliates bedeviled by the same infighting and hardships had never revolted. What separates them from the Islamic State of Iraq is also what explains its aberrant behavior: the group came to believe its own propaganda that it was, in fact, a state. Its flag—and not al Qaeda's—had become the symbol of the global jihad. Even al Qaeda's own affiliates flew it. Jihadist fanboys online counted the days since the state's establishment. And after the Islamic State began to control territory in 2012, it could truly claim to be a state in fact and not just in theory.

When, in 2013, the Islamic State (now calling itself the Islamic State of Iraq and al-Sham, or ISIS) proclaimed its authority over Syria and Iraq, Zawahiri demanded that it renounce that claim and return to Iraq. The response of ISIS' emir was dismissive: "I have chosen the command of my Lord over the command in the message that contradicts it." Months later, ISIS proclaimed itself the caliphate, rallying many in the global jihadist community to its side. It is far more exciting to be fighting for a caliphate that has returned than for a distant promise of its return under al Qaeda. Zawahiri's killer idea had taken on a life of its own, dismembering al Qaeda and replacing it as leader of the global jihad.

Despite ISIS' success in capturing jihadists' imagination, the idea of an Islamic state has one fatal flaw: its physical incarnation makes it vulnerable to attack. Take away the state's territory and expose its brutality and rapaciousness, and you discredit the standard-bearer of the idea. You may even discredit the idea itself. As Adnani prayed in a recent message, if this state is false, then may God "break its back . . . and guide its soldiers to the truth." The United States and its allies should do everything they can to ensure that the higher power does indeed destroy the state—and expose the truth.

The Women of ISIS

Understanding and Combating Female Extremism

Nimmi Gowrinathan

Reports that women have formed their own brigade within the Islamic State of Iraq and al-Sham (ISIS) have confounded experts—and worried them. For many, the idea of women as violent extremists seems paradoxical. After all, why should women want to join a political struggle that so blatantly oppresses them?

That question reveals more about the experts than the fighters. Those who ask it assume, first, that women are more peaceful than men by nature; and second, that women who participate in armed rebellion are little more than cannon fodder in a man's game, fighting foolishly for a movement that will not benefit them. As the women of ISIS prove, both assumptions are false.

To understand the women of ISIS and their motivations, it helps to place them in their historical context, among the legions of women in El Salvador, Eritrea, Nepal, Peru, and Sri Lanka who voluntarily joined violent movements and militias, sometimes even as highly ranked officers. In each of these cases, women joined for the same basic reasons as men. Living in deeply conservative social spaces, they faced constant threats to their ethnic, religious, or political identities—and it was typically those threats, rather than any grievances rooted in gender, that persuaded them to take up arms.

NIMMI GOWRINATHAN is a Fellow at the Center for Conflict, Negotiation and Recovery and the Gender Expert for the UN National Human Development Report in Afghanistan.

ISIS' particularly inhumane violence can obscure the fact that the conflict in Iraq is also rooted in identity: at its base, the fight is a sectarian struggle between Sunni and Shiite Muslims, with several smaller minorities caught in between. It makes sense, therefore, that the all-female al Khansaa Brigade of ISIS relies heavily on identity politics for recruitment, targeting young women who feel oppressed as Sunni Muslims. Indeed, anonymous fatwas calling for single women to join the fight for an Islamic caliphate have been attractive enough to draw women to ISIS from beyond the region.

If policymakers overlook such motivations, treating female fighters as nothing more than instruments of male leadership, they will find it difficult to prevent female extremism. As Jane Harman, president of the Woodrow Wilson International Center, wrote in a recent op-ed, countering radical narratives requires understanding the radicalized.

BEYOND GENDER

To be sure, for women, gender and politics can overlap in ways that they do not for men.

For most female fighters, the path to the battlefield is a brutal one. Many are driven to fight by a practical desire for safety. In war zones across the world, women absorb a disproportionate amount of the fallout from conflict, including material deprivation in refugee camps, daily harassment and fear in militarized zones, and a constant vulnerability to rape. Joining the fight is sometimes the only way to survive.

In 2005, I visited Sri Lanka to understand what drove women to join the Liberation Tigers of Tamil Eelam, a separatist terrorist group that sought an independent Tamil state on the island while also preserving culturally entrenched gender roles. For female commanders, security appeared to be a primary motivator. "The constant fear of living in militarized areas made me realize that life is unfair for Tamils," said one commander. (For safety reasons, the commanders declined to be named.) "So, I wanted to fight for equal rights."

Other female Tigers cited rape, or the fear of rape, by government forces as a central reason for joining the movement. As both a political act and a gendered one, rape is a unique motivator. "I was vulnerable because I was a woman, but I was targeted because I was a Tamil," said another female commander, reflecting the inherent difficulty of navigating between identities. Indeed, in the confusion of war, survival can depend on choosing which identity to prioritize. Tamil women, for example, often recognized the patriarchy of the Tamil movement yet still fought for it, tying their hopes for long-term security to a nationalist flag.

Consider the case of another Tamil commander I met, who spent her days patrolling local villages and posting leaflets that listed appropriate dress, hairstyle, and behavior for Tamil women: no short skirts, no short hair, no biking unless seated sideways. She herself sported combat boots and wore her hair short and closely cropped. I asked her how she reconciled the rules on the leaflets with her own decision to buck gender roles and take up arms. She said, "I fight to protect these values, to preserve the Tamil identity from being eliminated by the oppressor." The role of women thus becomes the anchor for the construction of a national identity.

At first glance, the experiences of women fighters in Sri Lanka seem to have little to do with the experiences of women fighters in Iraq, particularly because ISIS is so radically violent—reports have surfaced of ISIS soldiers slashing women's stomachs and burying children alive and so conservative toward women. But they are more similar to their counterparts in Sri Lanka and other conflict-ridden countries than they appear. As elsewhere, most Iraqi women take up arms because they fear for their safety or because they feel ISIS represents their political interests. In many cases, violence also appears to be the only available means of political expression. For many women, and especially for women from the marginalized Sunni community, violence becomes a vehicle for political agency.

ENDING EXTREMISM

To combat female extremism, the West must understand the grievances that motivate women to fight and then eliminate them. The usual fixes—providing financial or occupational support to young women and girls, for example—are unlikely to work, as women in war zones are deeply marginalized in every area of their lives. This sort of aid is important, of course, but it does not do enough: women in war zones, in addition to being poor, lack access to politics; and when they are unable to air their grievances publicly and nonviolently, extremism becomes more tempting.

Ironically, of course, female extremism rarely yields gains for women's rights. In Eritrea, for example, after the victory of the Eritrean People's Liberation Front, a secessionist movement in Ethiopia, female fighters were given control of social policy but had no real political voice. It appears likely that women in the envisioned Islamic State in Iraq will also be marginalized after the conflict ends.

If the West is ever to truly understand the women of ISIS, it must also reevaluate its preconceptions about gender and violence. In Iraq, Gaza, and elsewhere, the media are quick to paint women as victims and men as violent perpetrators. But that isn't always true. And this limited understanding of women's role in violence has implications beyond the conflict itself. Indeed, peacekeeping initiatives often leave women out of strategic discussions, relegating them to tasks explicitly concerning women's rights. This approach is unsustainable. In the end, peace is built through the inclusion of diverse perspectives, and so long as gendered assumptions persist, female voices will go unheard. Women fight for personal as well as political power, often sacrificing one for the other. If the world ignores that fact, it will miss a chance to deal with the identity politics that sustain war.

Syria's Democracy Jihad

Why ISIS Fighters Support the Vote

Vera Mironova, Loubna Mrie,
Richard Nielsen, and Sam Whitt

In the spring of 2011, it would have been impossible to predict that in Syria, in a few years' time, many of the pro-democracy activists who built a peaceful movement to bring down President Bashar al-Assad's dictatorship would be turning to jihadist groups that are now embroiled in the bloody civil war. Over the past year, the Free Syrian Army (FSA), once regarded as a force of moderate, secular democratic reformers, has partnered with—some members have even defected to—various moderate and radical Islamist groups, including the al Qaeda–linked al-Nusra Front and the Islamic State of Iraq and al-Sham (ISIS).

This trend is perplexing given the fundamentally incompatible values of jihadists and democratic revolutionaries, especially on the basics: human rights, tolerance, and political pluralism. To understand this paradox, we conducted a survey of 50 Islamist fighters from Ahrar al-Sham and al-Nusra, along with several sheiks, who were educated in Saudi Arabia. These surveys were

VERA MIRONOVA is a doctoral candidate at the University of Maryland.

LOUBNA MRIE is a Syrian journalist.

RICHARD NIELSEN is Assistant Professor of Political Science at the Massachusetts Institute of Technology.

SAM WHITT is Assistant Professor of Political Science at High Point University in North Carolina.

conducted as part of our broader Voices of Syria project, which includes over 500 interviews with Syrian civilians, rebel fighters, and refugees in Syria and Turkey. In order to safely conduct interviews with Ahrar al-Sham and al-Nusra fighters in Idlib, our interviewer had to seek permission from the informal Islamic court that has jurisdiction over the territory occupied by those particular brigades. All interviews were conducted face-to-face, privately, and anonymously.

Based on our research in Syria from late April to early May 2014, the Islamist fighters we interviewed were surprisingly supportive of democracy. In the long-besieged province of Idlib, about 40 miles west of Aleppo, we found that 60 percent of the Islamist fighters we interviewed from Ahrar al-Sham and the al Qaeda–affiliated al-Nusra agreed that "democracy is preferable to any other form of governance." Further, 78 percent of these Islamists also strongly agreed that "it is essential for Syria to remain a unified state," which seems to contradict the goal of building a more encompassing Islamic caliphate. Although this finding may seem at odds with the theocratic aims of Islamist groups, we suspect that Islamists are rethinking their position on democracy in order to widen their ideological net and recruit more fighters.

Baffling as it seems, transforming pro-democracy activists into radical jihadists is neither impossible nor completely illogical. The Syrian revolution began as an anti-Assad, pro-democracy movement, and its most active participants drew inspiration from the moderate uprisings in Tunisia and Egypt. But when Assad began brutally suppressing the protests, many Syrians either fled the country or turned to groups fighting under the banner of the FSA, which aspired toward a unified, democratic Syria.

With the Syrian civil war in its third year, however, the FSA has been unable to fulfill its revolutionary promise. Its forces have been decimated by the combined onslaughts of well-financed jihadist groups and an Assad regime reinvigorated by the lack of Western intervention and staunch support from Russia and Iran. The FSA's corruption, infighting, and poor organizational capacity have also significantly eroded the trust and confidence of its soldiers, many of whom have left.

For Islamic brigades, the FSA's fragmentation has presented an opportunity to draw new members into their own ranks by demonstrating that their leadership skills, organization, and resources have allowed the groups to succeed in battle where the FSA could not. Some former FSA fighters we interviewed switched to Islamist groups not out of inspiration for jihad, but because of poor fighting conditions inside the FSA. "I was with my old group [FSA] until I fought with Ahrar al-Sham," stated one former FSA fighter. "I liked their way of treating fighters, so I joined." In particular, Islamist groups are seen to provide better care for injured fighters. One rebel fighter who switched from the FSA to Ahrar al-Sham told us, "My friend got injured and they [FSA] didn't support him." Second, the Islamists pandered to moderate skeptics by emphasizing their common cause—the removal of Assad—and downplaying their desire for an Islamic state, leading new converts to believe that Syria's future would be decided by its people.

Indeed, 94 percent of the Islamist rebel fighters we interviewed have retained their revolutionary goals to defeat the Assad regime. And only a quarter of the ostensibly "Islamist" rebels claimed that their goal is "to build an Islamic state" in Syria. This finding suggests that many rank-and-file fighters may have purely strategic motives in fighting under an Islamist banner—they just want to see Assad go.

For Islamist groups, this pool of committed fighters is but a fleeting advantage. As long as Islamists remain committed to liberating Syria from Assad, the rebels will fight with them. But if the war is won, the Syrian rebels may not commit to the broader principles of jihad or show any interest in building an Islamic state. To try to prevent that from happening, Islamist groups have invested heavily in the reeducation of new recruits through daily religious lectures delivered not by fellow Syrians but by sheiks trained in Saudi Arabia.

This strategy seems to be paying off. Nearly three-quarters of the Islamist fighters we surveyed claimed to have grown more religious since the war began. "Under the Assad regime, we did not know true Islam, but after the revolution, the hardship we experienced forced us to be closer to God," explained one Syrian fighter who joined the FSA but later switched to al-Nusra. "Religion gives us inner peace, which is exactly what we need now in the war zone, when everyone left us." Taking advantage of the rebels' generally low levels of education and cursory understanding of democracy, Islamist lecturers condemn the evils of Western-style democracy and tout the benefits of an Islamic state. The fatal flaw in Western democracy, they argue, is the separation of state and religion, which they portray as an absolute prohibition of religious practice; and in the absence of sharia law, corruption, prostitution, drug use, and other vices flourish. The sheiks also teach that Western secularism is responsible for Assad's corruption and brutality. As one sheik explained, "Assad is committing crimes because he is secular, and he is secular because of Western influence." Another sheik explained to us in a private interview:

> "Democracy has had it all wrong from the very beginning. I have read about and researched [the origins of] democracy. Democracy is itself a kind of crazy religion, where the people are given the control, ruling the country through elections. Elections existed in the old days of Islam, but only the virtuous people in society—those with good reputations—were allowed to vote. But in today's world, people have become corrupt. If we ask these people to vote, to elect someone to be in charge, then they will choose the biggest thief among themselves. That's why I am against democracy, against rule by the people. Democracy, in today's sense, is bad because it does not encourage people to live by sharia law."

It is currently unclear how the Islamists' version of democracy might work in practice. But according to the sheik quoted above, it might offer candidates the choice of opting out of certain Islamic practices but offer incentives to opt in. The sheik explained his idea of religious freedom with the following example: "When al-Nusra took control of Idlib, they said that girls will have a choice at school whether to wear the *niqab* or not. But if they want to wear it, the school will provide the *niqab* for free." By incorporating themes of liberation from tyranny into jihadist rhetoric, Islamist groups have successfully appealed to moderate supporters of the Syrian revolution. Since the average Syrian has at best vague notions of democracy, having lived only under dictatorial rule, co-opting democratic values for jihadist purposes is not as odd as it might seem: both democratic and jihadist movements have historically involved bloody uprisings that seek to overturn prior political and social orders.

Finally, by reframing the struggle for jihad as a quest to preserve the right of religious expression, Islamist groups have also bolstered their recruitment efforts inside Western democracies. We interviewed four foreign fighters who came from Saudi Arabia, France, Russia, and Algeria. As one of them remarked, "Democracy is freedom and in particular freedom of opinion and choice. So I personally choose al-Nusra."

Blood Money

How ISIS Makes Bank

Louise Shelley

A key element of U.S. President Barack Obama's strategy against the Islamic State of Iraq and al-Sham (ISIS) has been striking at the oil fields seized by the group to undermine its finances. But ISIS is a diversified criminal business, and oil is only one of its several revenue streams. U.S. officials ignore that fact at their own peril.

It is true that oil is ISIS' key source of funding right now. The terrorist group has become the world's richest precisely because it has seized some of the world's most profitable oil fields in Iraq and Syria. Even with those fields operating below capacity due to a lack of technology and personnel, ISIS is estimated to be producing about 44,000 barrels a day in Syria and 4,000 barrels a day in Iraq. ISIS sells crude at a discount (around $20–$35 per barrel) to either truckers or middlemen. The crude gets to refiners at around $60 per barrel, which is still under market price. Smugglers pay about $5,000 in bribes at checkpoints to move the crude oil out of ISIS controlled territory. Even selling the oil at a discount via pre-invasion smuggling routes out of Iraq, ISIS can still expect over a million dollars in revenue each day.

And ISIS' enemies are getting richer from the trade, too: Kurdish part-time smugglers who facilitate ISIS' oil sales can earn up to $300,000 each month. A Kurdish newspaper recently published a

LOUISE SHELLEY is University Professor at George Mason University and Director of the Terrorism, Transnational Crime, and Corruption Center (TraCCC). She is the author of *Dirty Entanglements: Corruption, Crime, and Terrorism*.

list of people involved with ISIS, especially its oil operations. The list includes individuals with the last names of several Kurdish ruling families; a Toyota branch in Erbil, which sells ISIS trucks; a Politburo member and military leader; and oil refineries, among others. Some of those on the list were associated with oil smuggling under Saddam Hussein. Kurdish facilitators also provide goods to ISIS, including trucks, gas cylinders (for cooking and heating), gasoline, and other necessary commodities.

Oil is not ISIS' only source of revenue. For example, when the group needed seed capital to recruit personnel and acquire military equipment to conquer the Sunni-dominated areas of Iraq, some of it came from donors in the Gulf States, who had funded the antecedents of ISIS. More recently, ISIS funding has come from the usual terrorist businesses—smuggling, kidnapping, extortion, and robberies. In one reported case, a Swedish company paid $70,000 to rescue an employee who had been taken by ISIS. And before the American journalist James Foley was beheaded, ISIS fighters demanded an exorbitant sum for his freedom, which they did not receive.

Still more funding comes from the sale of counterfeit cigarettes, pharmaceuticals, cell phones, antiquities, and foreign passports. The trafficking of some of these commodities into Turkey from Syria has risen dramatically. For example, cigarette smuggling has increased, fuel smuggling is estimated to have tripled, and cell phone smuggling has risen fivefold. ISIS is also taxing black market antiquities at 20–50 percent, depending on the region and type of antiquity. Meanwhile, foreign fighters sell their passports for thousands of dollars in Turkey before entering Syria, where the proceeds help fund them and ISIS. These particular forms of illicit trade are attractive to terrorists because there is less competition, less regulation, and limited law enforcement in these markets compared to others, such as the arms and narcotics trades.

These days, ISIS in many ways resembles a legitimate business. It has diverse revenue sources, seeks and develops new profit lines, and focuses on its most successful products and competitive advantages. ISIS was smuggling oil in Syria before its fighters entered Iraq. The lure of those better oil fields might have been one of the reasons it expanded its operations. ISIS is also entrepreneurial—for example, it has obtained several modular mini-refineries, which are low cost, low capacity, and mobile. The U.S. Department of Defense has targeted about a dozen of these facilities. ISIS leaders are rational business actors, too. They seek the best professional services; engage in cost-benefit analysis, focusing on crimes that yield the highest reward with the lowest risk; and use advanced technology to recruit personnel globally.

ISIS leaders' talent for business is not surprising. Although the group has its fair share of ideological fanatics, it also includes foreign fighters that have extensive criminal expertise, such as the Georgian militant Tarkhan Batirashvili, known by his nom de guerre Sheikh Abu Omar al-Shishani, who was arrested for illegally harboring weapons. Of ISIS leader Abu Bakr al-Baghdadi's 25 deputies in Iraq and Syria, approximately a third served in the military during Saddam Hussein's rule, and nearly all were imprisoned by American forces after the 2003 invasion, often with terrorists and insurgents who are now in ISIS. These experienced Baathists can tap into the illicit smuggling networks of the Saddam era.

In other words, ISIS already had years of expertise in outsmarting the West as it establishes front companies, bribes officials, and launders money. And, with its greatest revenue stream—oil—under attack, it can easily adjust the balance of its portfolio to favor non-oil activity. What's more, now that the group actually controls territory, it can squeeze the local population and businesses for cash and taxes, just as the Taliban did to great effect in Afghanistan.

The United States and other governments, expecting strikes on ISIS-held oil facilities to be a silver bullet, have failed to adequately engage the business community, which could provide enormous insight into ISIS' operations. To undermine an economic competitor, you must do more than cut off its key funding—you have to go after its business and business models. In other words, it takes business to defeat an illicit business.

To prevent firms in Kurdish Iraq from selling trucks to ISIS or helping refine oil, the West could do more to ensure that the government in Baghdad pays good prices for the oil that it is obtaining from Kurdish Iraq and shares its revenues with the region. The failure of the central government to do so means that businesses will seek alternative customers—even bad ones.

The effort to counter ISIS should also involve Western businesses. The cigarette industry follows the ebb and flow of the illicit cigarette trade. Energy and pharmaceutical companies monitor the movement of their commodities in the region. Transport companies have insights into the dynamics of illicit trade, and insurance companies have insights into kidnapping. That is why public-private partnerships are key. Corporations can share the information they already collect on illicit trade routes, smuggling shipments, and key facilitators. They can also warn consumers not to purchase the counterfeit and smuggled commodities that fund terrorism.

For now, the government response to ISIS has not taken the business community enough into account. But without such cooperation, Washington cannot hope to successfully counter the nimble ISIS.

ISIS Sends a Message

What Gestures Say About Today's Middle East

Nathaniel Zelinsky

Amasked man brandishes a severed head in one hand. In the other, he raises an index finger, a commonly understood symbol for the number one.

His name is Abdel Majed Abdel Bary, a failed London rapper turned jihadist, a British militant fighting for the Islamic State of Iraq and al-Sham (ISIS), also known as the Islamic State. British authorities suspect him of murdering American journalists Steven Sotloff and James Foley. In August, Bary posted a gruesome picture—from a different killing—on his Twitter account for the world to see.

The curious thing was not the head Bary held in his left hand—however ghoulish the trophy—but the gesture he made with his right. For followers of ISIS, a single raised index finger has become a sign of their cause, and it is increasingly common in photographs of militants. Some have even gone so far as to call the symbol "the jihadi equivalent of a gang sign."

The Middle East and its upheavals are no strangers to gestures. Over the past year, a variety of groups, ranging from the Muslim Brotherhood in Egypt to the Kurds in Iraq, have used at least four distinct hand signals. These symbols communicate complex political messages that Western observers have largely ignored. That

NATHANIEL ZELINSKY is a Paul Mellon Scholar at Clare College, the University of Cambridge.

lapse is certainly understandable: next to a severed head, the number one is easy to overlook.

Yet gestures—in particular ISIS' index finger—should demand far more attention. They are an important means by which regional groups communicate their core messages to viewers down the street and observers thousands of miles away in Europe and the United States. To understand the ideologies such groups aim to export, one needs to understand the symbols they use.

SIGNALS INTELLIGENCE

Gestures are as old as politics itself. They became especially important, however, with the advent of mass media in the twentieth century. Consider what is perhaps the best-known example: Adolf Hitler's fascist salute. In a single gesture, Hitler communicated the power of National Socialism, the obedience of German crowds, and his own role as a supreme leader. And because pictures of him saluting were printed in newspapers around the world, the symbol reached billions.

Each subsequent advance in media technology has made it easier for political messages to reach mass audiences. But the Internet changed the rules of the game, democratizing the entire process of image making. Today, anyone with a cell phone can broadcast an image in an instant—which is exactly what Bary did.

When ISIS militants hold up a single index finger on their right hands, they are alluding to the *tawhid*, the belief in the oneness of God and a key component of the Muslim religion. The *tawhid* comprises the first half of the *shahada*, which is an affirmation of faith, one of the five pillars of Islam, and a component of daily prayers: "There is no god but Allah, Muhammad is the messenger of Allah."

It is no surprise, then, that the *shahada* features prominently in ISIS' public image. The group's black flag bears the vow's words in white Arabic script (as does Hamas' and even Saudi Arabia's). And Muslims have long associated a single index finger with the *shahada* in a variety of contexts, ranging from daily prayers to conversions.

But for ISIS, the symbol is more sinister than a mere declaration of monotheistic beliefs. As Salafi jihadists, members of the group adhere to a fundamentalist interpretation of *tawhid* that rejects non-fundamentalist regimes as idolatrous. In other words, the concept of *tawhid* is central to ISIS' violent and uncompromising posture toward its opponents, both in the Middle East and in the West.

When ISIS militants display the sign, to one another or to a photographer, they are actively reaffirming their dedication to that ideology, whose underlying principle demands the destruction of the West. If rank-and-file soldiers are aware of the precise theological implications of their sign—and it would be no surprise if they are—that would be a sobering comment on their deep-seated opposition to pluralism.

The gesture is equally important for what it means to Westerners, most of whom cannot read Arabic. By raising their index fingers, militants send an easy-to-understand message of the group's goals of theological supremacy and military hegemony. When potential ISIS recruits in London, New York, or Sydney see the symbol on Twitter, they can grasp the scale of ISIS' ambitions and its underlying aims. At some visceral level, less-radicalized viewers understand that it means dominance.

If ISIS has the solitary finger, its opponents have the so-called V-for-Victory gesture, popular among Iraqi soldiers and the Kurdish militia. Originally devised by the British Broadcasting Corporation as a sign of the Allied powers during World War II, the V has been used in the Middle East since its creation in 1941. At various moments in history, a wide array of groups has appropriated the symbol, among them Palestinian terrorists, Iranians who took part in the failed "green revolution," and Egyptians in Tahrir Square.

As the diversity of its devotees suggests, the V has less rigidly defined political dimensions than the raised finger. It is a general symbol of defiance, protest, and self-expression without intellectual meaning. (The V is so generic, in fact, that supporters of ISIS have also displayed it in photographs.) But in some ways, the use of the V cuts to the core of what the opposition to ISIS is all about—a collection of factions with differing aims and worldviews bound together only by a fear of the Islamic State. Whereas ISIS' followers are unified by fundamentalist ideals, its opponents are not equally united.

FREEDOM OF GESTURE

ISIS and its opponents are not the only groups in the region making use of gestures. Two other symbols have been visible in the region over the past year, and they provide important context for ISIS' index finger signal.

One gesture emerged when Hamas operatives kidnapped three Israeli teenagers last July. Palestinians celebrated the news by jubilantly thrusting three fingers in the air, one for each of the hostages Israel would have to ransom by releasing convicted terrorists from jail. Called the "three Shalits," after the IDF-soldier-turned-hostage Gilad Shalit, the symbol quickly spread across the Arab world via social media, in many cases with young children posing for the camera and proudly showing three fingers.

As with ISIS' signal, this new gesture's intended message was easy to comprehend: ordinary Palestinians supported Hamas and its tactics. However, where Western media has been slow to identify the significance of ISIS' sigil, the Israeli press and some U.S. media outlets quickly highlighted the meaning and implications of the "three Shalits." At one level, the difference in responses is not surprising: the pro-Hamas symbol appeared across the West Bank and was a more immediate concern to Israel, physically and politically, than ISIS' gesture seems to be to the West.

The second symbol, championed by the Muslim Brotherhood in Egypt, was widespread a year ago, but has since begun to disappear. Last summer, Mohammed Morsi, who was president of Egypt, clashed with the country's army in a contest that ended with his fall from power. In one incident, the army killed hundreds of Morsi's followers at the Rabaa al-Adawiya mosque. The word Rabaa means "four" in Egypt, and the Brotherhood quickly adopted a four-fingered hand gesture as its symbol.

In rallies from Cairo to Istanbul, Brotherhood supporters held up yellow signs with a Rabaa hand-gesture printed in black, wore Rabaa buttons, and made the signal with their own hands. It was an attempt to remind Egyptians and the world of the Army's massacre and shift the narrative away from Morsi's failed democratic promises.

Since the Egyptian army deposed Morsi, it has worked hard to quash the Rabaa, banning the country's Olympic athletes from making the gesture in Sochi this past winter. The Brotherhood's supporters, meanwhile, have tried to keep it alive, hosting a worldwide "Rabaa day" this past August. The army's efforts seem to be paying off, as the gesture and its underlying message are petering out somewhat from the international stage. If the Rabaa is a bellwether for the health of the Muslim Brotherhood, don't bet on the group returning to power any time soon.

For governments in the West, the Rabaa should raise an important question: When ISIS' index finger reaches their shores, do they follow the Egyptian model of suppression? Or do they honor principles of free expression? Dilemmas of free speech, of course, are nothing new. European authorities have grappled with a similar question with regard to the so-called quenelle, an anti-Semitic gesture that resembles a reversed Hitler salute. French officials have taken a hard line, attempting to bar the comedian Dieudonne M'bala M'bala, who invented the quenelle, from performing in the country. The French Football Association has disciplined soccer players for displaying the quenelle in matches. But it seems that attempting to suppress the gesture has been far from effective, turning Dieudonne into a martyr for free expression.

Middle Eastern gestures, meanwhile, have already made their way west. In some cases, they have met with censorship: Facebook took down a public group that encouraged users to upload photos expressing support for kidnappings carried out by Hamas with a three-fingered salute. If any gesture were to be banned, it would be the raised index finger, which already cropped up at a pro-ISIS rally in The Hague at the end of July. However, measures to criminalize ISIS' hallmark would, as in the case of the quenelle, likely backfire, turning ISIS supporters into victims of censorship.

At the very least, Westerners need to become more attuned to what the gesture means. It is doubtful that most Dutch citizens understood the radical ideas behind the raised index fingers in The Hague, and one could say the same of publics in other Western countries. Their continued ignorance will only make it more difficult to evaluate the threat ISIS poses in the Middle East.

ISIS' single raised digit, so seemingly inconsequential at first blush, is a statement about the group's diametric opposition to a liberal world order. Its use is all the more troubling in the hands of Western-born Jihadists with the passports to travel outside the Middle East. Indeed, those who underestimate the dangers posed by the Islamic State need look no further than the index finger, which makes ISIS' ambitions all too clear.

Securing al-Sham

Syria and the Violence in Iraq

Andrew J. Tabler

Uprooting the Islamic State of Iraq and al Sham (ISIS) from the swath of territory it now holds between Aleppo and Baghdad will take a lot more than airstrikes or a change of government in Iraq. Although the 2003 war in Iraq might have led to the formation of the jihadi group, the chaos in Syria provided it the space to metastasize. To prevent ISIS—and other such organizations—from building a permanent safe haven in Iraq and Syria, then, Washington must help settle Syria by supporting Sunni tribes and other moderate opposition groups there.

FRACTURED FRONT

Over the last week, the Obama administration has focused its attention on pushing Iraqi Prime Minister Nouri al-Maliki (or whoever might replace him) to be more inclusive of the country's Sunni Arabs, who make up around 20 percent of the population. Washington is right to do so. ISIS and the other groups fighting alongside it rely on this disenchanted community for support. Without Sunni backing, ISIS would crumble and Iraq could stabilize. To help that process along, the United States could launch airstrikes against ISIS camps in the country.

Sunni Arabs are an even larger part of the equation in Syria, where they represent between 65 and 70 percent of the population

ANDREW J. TABLER is senior fellow at the Washington Institute for Near East Policy and author of *In the Lion's Den: An Eyewitness Account of Washington's Battle with Syria*. Follow him on Twitter @andrewtabler.

and make up the backbone of the opposition to the Alawite Assad regime. Western mediators have urged Assad to negotiate with Alawites, Shia, and Sunnis. But he has refused, preferring instead to have himself "re-elected" to a third term as president and to make vague promises of dialogue with the opposition groups that succumb to the regime's siege-and-starve tactics.

Assad might seem like he is in control, but his troops rarely tangle with ISIS, preferring instead to take on the more moderate factions. In fact, his regime has only been able to go on the offensive in western Syria with help from Hezbollah, Iraqi Shia militias, and Iran's Quds force. When their support disappears, so, too, will Assad's luck. For example, when Iraqi Shia militiamen were recently recalled from the Lebanese-Syrian frontier to fight ISIS in Iraq, Syrian opposition forces quickly reappeared, retook part of the area, and continued to stage hit-and-run attacks. In other words, Assad and the rebels are at a stalemate and, unless the West and its Arab allies try something new, the conflict will persist.

BORDERLANDS

The best way to permanently uproot ISIS is to follow the example of Jordan. In recent years, Jordan has relied on a two-part strategy to deal with the Syrian crisis: control the border with Syria and monitor and work with the Syrian opposition to keep radical rebel groups out of the country's southern reaches, along the border with Jordan. The U.S. intelligence community, which has a close relationship with Jordan, has reportedly participated in this effort.

Moderate groups continue to hold their own in southern Syria, but, as in other areas of the country, they still rely on coordination with more radical groups to fight the Assad regime. To prevent those radical groups from spilling into Jordan, Amman closed one of its border crossings to refugees and reopened it further east, in uncontested territory. It also worked with Western intelligence agencies to increase covert support for moderate groups in southern Syria. As a result, ISIS has yet to take root there.

For Turkey to strengthen its own border with northern Syria, it would have to follow Jordan's example. So far, though, Ankara has been reluctant to get as strict about people, money, and weapons crossing its frontier into and out of Syria. There is considerable risk that militants could retaliate against Turkey if it decided to clamp down, but surely the Syrians roaming its territory already present such a risk. To help Turkey make the right call, the United States could promise to use drones or airstrikes to help Turkey secure the border.

After closing the borders between Syria and Jordan and Syria and Turkey, it will be time to address the now-gaping border between Syria and Iraq. The best way to do that is by working with tribes in the area and with selective drone strikes. Sunni tribal confederations such as the Baggara, Dulaim, Jabbour, N'eim, Qugaidat, Shammar, and Tai'e extend into Syria and Iraq—and some even reach into Qatar, Saudi Arabia, and the United Arab Emirates. These tribes could be made into a bulwark against ISIS and other jihadists in Syria and Iraq. According to some reports, ISIS has worked to win over their rank and file by offering basic services. For those that don't accept such carrots, the group has used harsh sticks, such as beheadings and crucifixions. Its pull among the tribal population worries local tribal leaders, who see their influence slipping.

Arab intelligence agencies can play on these fears by supplying tribal leaders with lethal and nonlethal assistance. The United States is not in a good position to lead this effort, since it has no boots on the ground and lacks the qualitative intelligence. However, Washington should coordinate closely with Arab Gulf countries in supporting tribes against militant groups, using air power to aid their fight against ISIS.

Another natural bulwark against ISIS and other such groups is Syria's Kurdish population in northeast Syria. To stave off the militant threat, the Kurds united two years ago under the banner of the Kurdish Supreme Committee. The group includes the radical Democratic Union Party of Syria, which is the Syrian offshoot of the Kurdistan Workers' Party, and the more moderate Kurdistan National Council, an alliance of 15 Kurdish political parties. Despite tensions among its members, the alliance has battled jihadists for the better part of two years. And like their Arab counterparts, the Kurds are also organized into broad tribal confederations that reach across the border into Iraq and Turkey.

Sealing off Syria's external borders—and its internal one with the Kurdish region—would help contain jihadist groups and interdict ISIS suicide operators coming to Iraq while the United States works with the Iraqi government to win over moderate Sunnis and, possibly, launches drone strikes against ISIS positions. This could be bolstered through the creation of a U.S. Joint Special Operations Task Force to coordinate cross-border operations. Meanwhile, allying with the Arab tribes on both sides of the border will undermine ISIS support in its key Sunni Arab demographic. This could result in a foreign policy twofer, helping address both the current situation in Iraq and Syria and the broader jihadist threat over the long term.

SYRIAN SOLUTION

With ISIS hemmed in, the crisis in Iraq would be far easier to manage through airstrikes and diplomacy.

The world could then turn to the war in Syria. The top-down diplomatic efforts to resolve the crisis are going nowhere. According to Samantha Power, U.S. representative to the United Nations, more Syrian civilians died from Assad's barrel bombs during this year's failed peace talks in Geneva than during any other period in the Syrian war. And that onslaught continues to this day. The best way to keep the regime from dropping barrel bombs, as well as chlorine gas and other indiscriminate weapons, would be to shoot down its aircraft.

Providing vetted armed groups with antiaircraft weapons would help the opposition secure its territory. It would also empower moderates by making them key to defending against Assad's onslaught. Although antiaircraft guns would not take care of the regime's weapon of choice—artillery—civilians would at least have less reason to flee to Turkey and Jordan, which are already overwhelmed with refugees and fear spillover violence. The United States could provide the opposition active intelligence to facilitate such operations.

Now the question is how to channel antiaircraft and other heavy weapons so that they don't fall into radicals' hands. Much has been made of the bickering and petty rivalries within the Syrian National Coalition (SNC) and the thousand or so armed groups fighting against the Assad regime. The divisions are partly a reflection of Syria's extremely diverse Sunni population—from the urbane Sunnis representing the traditional elites, who long collaborated with the regime, to the tribal Sunnis of eastern Syria and Dera, who cooperated with the regime at arm's length, to the conservative Sunnis of northwestern Syria, who have long fought Alawites and the Assad regime. ISIS and other militant groups, such as the al Qaeda affiliate Jabhat al-Nusra, are primarily entrenched within the tribal and conservative Sunni populations.

The Supreme Military Council (SMC), an umbrella organization that Arab and Western intelligence helped set up in late 2012 as the armed wing of the SNC, was meant to unify rebels' supply chains, encourage moderates to unite, and empower the SNC on the ground. Unfortunately, it hasn't worked, which coalition leaders blame on a lack of outside support. The problem with the SMC is that, like the SNC, it is beset with petty rivalries and has at times been infiltrated by radical Salafis. For that reason, it would be unwise to use the SMC, at least as it exists now, to channel antiaircraft weapons to moderate rebels.

The other major conduit supporting the rebels has been individual groups vetted by Western and Arab intelligence agencies, including the Syrian Revolutionary Front and Harakat Hazm, which have been given American-made antitank missiles. Such vetted groups stand wholly apart from their more radical counterparts, but their lack of resources or political agenda has hobbled them. The SMC leadership, moreover, has criticized Western efforts to supply some groups with weapons as creating warlordism among the moderate Syrian opposition.

But given the threat that jihadist groups pose in Syria, selective arming seems like the least bad option. And antiaircraft weapons would come with strings attached. In the short term, the regional intelligence agencies that are advising moderate groups inside Syria would be best placed to carry out joint antiaircraft operations until the moderate Syrian opposition can stand on its own. Over the longer term, the SMC should be reconstituted as a clear anti-radical force with more tribal leaders and leaders from vetted groups. As was the clear during the SMC's initial formation, Arab and Western intelligence agencies are best placed carry out the task. A new SMC could be the channel for other heavy weapons as well and the conduit for setting up governments in opposition areas coordinated with the SNC and other groups in exile.

Eventually, as the SMC's capabilities increase, the group could fill vacuums in areas where ISIS and other jihadi groups give way. Eventually, the SMC would fully train its sights on the Assad regime. Assad, in turn, would come to appreciate that his military solution to the Syria conflict is doomed to fail and that he needs to return to the negotiating table.

PAYING UP

For the second time in less than a year, U.S. President Barack Obama is considering military strikes in the Middle East. Targeted air, missile, and drone attacks could degrade ISIS' capabilities and should be used carefully. But they will not fix the region's problems—especially the ongoing war between the Tigris and Euphrates rivers.

The United States must start to address those problems by increasing covert support for border security operations and for the Syrian opposition. To do so, it can tap the $5 billion Counterterrorism Partnerships Fund that Obama recently outlined in a speech at West Point. This fund aims to expand the training and equipping of foreign militaries, bolster allied counterterrorism capabilities, and support efforts to counter violence extremism and terrorist ideology.

Yet Syrians cannot unite around groups armed in the shadows. A much more comprehensive and overt training and equipping program, as recently introduced in the National Defense Authorization Act, would help the United States build up moderate forces in Syria that could effectively combat Assad and deescalate the crisis. Although it is still unclear which moderate Sunni oppositionists will be part of any final negotiated settlement, it is clear is that ISIS and other radicals can't be included.

Radical Turks

Why Turkish Citizens are Joining ISIS

Gunes Murat Tezcur and Sabri Ciftci

The past few weeks have seen a wave of Muslims from all around the world joining the ranks of the Islamic State of Iraq and al-Sham (ISIS). Although most of the attention has been on those coming from the United States and Europe, the bulk of foreign fighters has actually come from Algeria, Morocco, Saudi Arabia, Tunisia, and Turkey.

The flow of jihadists from Turkey is particularly puzzling. For one, in the past, Turkish citizens have not joined jihadist groups such as al Qaeda in large numbers. In addition, ISIS advances in Iraq and Syria have come at a high cost to the Turkish people. During the assault on the Syrian Kurdish town of Kobani in October, for example, Turkish Kurds took to the street in large numbers, protesting Ankara's inaction. Riots left around 50 people dead. More than a thousand buildings, including schools, banks, health centers, and administrative offices, were burned to the ground. Business confidence in the Kurdish provinces was severely undermined. Finally, the appeal of radicalism is hard to square with Turkey's image as a role model of Muslim democracy. The country has a history of electoral democracy going back to 1950, longer than any other Muslim-majority nation in the world, and has been ruled by a moderate Islamist party since 2002. Theorists have long

GUNES MURAT TEZCUR is Associate Professor of Political Science at the Loyola University Chicago.

SABRI CIFTCI is Assistant Professor of Political Science at Kansas State University.

posited that Islamist political participation would diminish radicalism as Islamists become stakeholders in the existing system.

In fact, radicalization in Turkey is peculiarly suited to the evolution in recent years of the country's civil society and political institutions under the ruling Justice and Development Party (AKP)—and, in turn, the types of Turks who have been caught up in the jihadist net make for unusual recruits.

SIGN UP

According to recent reports, around 1,000 Turkish citizens have joined ISIS and several hundred have joined Jabhat al Nusra, the al Qaeda branch in Syria. These numbers likely underestimate the real scope of jihadist mobilization in Turkey, owing to the weak patrolling along the Turkish-Syrian border. To get a better sense of who these fighters are, we generated a new database with information on about 112 individuals who joined the jihadists. We used open sources such as newspapers, magazines, online news portals, forums, and blogs to collect biographical information. We also visited Turkey and attended Islamic circles with pro-jihadist views to develop a better understanding of the conditions under which Turks radicalize.

The data set reveals several interesting patterns. The jihadists, who are all males, come from diverse social and economic backgrounds. They include lawyers, merchants, small-shop owners, university students, and government and private service employees. A surprisingly high number of them are married. Among the records we have, 31 are married with children and 37 are not married. The average educational attainment of the group is higher than the national average, and many of the recruits have stable jobs. The average age at the time of joining the jihad was 27, significantly older than Kurdish nationalist fighters in Turkey and Syria. Although the jihadists have diverse geographic and ethnic origins, Kurds are overrepresented in the sample. Many of the Kurds in Turkey traveled to Syria to fight against ISIS, but many others joined ISIS or other Islamist organizations Close to 50 percent of the sample, 51 recruits, are of

Kurdish ethnicity. About a third of the fighters are veterans of earlier jihadist wars in Bosnia, Chechnya, Afghanistan, and Iraq. Seventeen of them had court records for their Islamic activities. Most of the rest, though, have no history of political activism.

These characteristics are surprising. Most of the literature on radicalization highlights the role of relative deprivation, the lack of a robust Muslim middle class, social networks that alienate young Muslims from the rest of the society, or victimization at the hands of repressive state authorities. But many of the Turkish fighters have stable family structures and are embedded in strong communal networks. Further, with Turkey having been ruled by an Islamist party for the last 12 years, most of the current fighters would have little or no direct experience of state religious repression. Unlike other countries in the region, moreover, Turkey has an expanding economy that has lifted large numbers of its citizens out of poverty. Although inequality among groups has not necessarily diminished, most Turkish citizens have become better off during the AKP era. And many of those who joined the jihad in Syria benefited from the increasing wealth.

In other words, when it comes to radicalism in Turkey, something very unusual is going on.

THE TURKISH FAITH

According to conventional interpretations, Islam in Turkey stands as distinct from Salafi Islam in the rest of the region because Turkish Islamic movements have favored moderate and pragmatic rhetoric—and active accommodation of Westernism and secularism—to win a space for religion in public and political life. The 1990s saw the rise of several violent Islamist groups in response to the Turkish military's authoritarian secularism, but their appeal remained very limited. The rise of the ruling AKP and Gulen movement came to epitomize the possibility of a new Muslim model of governance incorporating piety, pluralism, secularism, and moderation.

Over the course of its rule, the AKP has achieved impressive economic growth rates after a decade of economic mismanagement and political instability. Pious Muslims, who previously felt like second-class citizens, embraced AKP rule, which put them at the top of the hierarchy. For a long time, and especially after the Arab uprisings of 2011, the "Turkish model" appeared to offer a way out of the vicious cycle of authoritarian rule and illiberal Islamist populism that beset many Middle Eastern regimes.

Yet AKP rule came with some unintended consequences. For one, it led to much more civic activism overall, because AKP sponsored Islamic organizations both to please its core supporters and to promote a more pious society. And that burst of activism facilitated radicalization, because organizations had free rein to pursue their own intolerant and exclusive agendas as long as they did not challenge the AKP. The process has accelerated with President Recep Tayyip Erdogan's increasing monopolization of power. Press freedom has been in constant decline, judicial independence has been curtailed, and security services use disproportionate force against protesters and the like. Even as the institutions central to democratic functioning have eroded, Islamic activism has continued to flourish with few checks.

Both institutional (registered organizations) and informal (conversation groups, street gatherings, café groups, mosque groups) types of Islamic activism have expanded. In our fieldwork in Turkey, we found that jihadists exploited the freer civil space provided by the AKP to form conversation groups, turn bookstores into social centers, and recruit in mosques. For example, over 180 religious publishing houses and bookstores participated in a record-setting book fair during Ramadan in Istanbul. *Iftars* (Ramadan dinners) and the special *tarawih* prayers organized by religious groups, including those with ISIS sympathies, provided an environment for radicals to network. The increasing numbers of Syrian refugees brutalized by a vicious civil war provided an additional impetus to join up.

Overall, a flourishing civil society and decaying political institutions have created a radical-friendly environment in Turkey. And that presents a challenge to conventional thinking about the mutually reinforcing link between civil society, moderation, and democracy. Civil society has a dark side, and it might undermine democracy when that democracy doesn't have strong checks and balances. This is particularly true in the informal sphere, where ad hoc and semi-clandestine networks compete with the government for loyalty.

This unique constellation of conditions in Turkey has contributed to the radicalization of educated and socially well-connected individuals. And that will make it all the harder to curb the appeal of jihadism. In fact, there is likely no silver bullet to the problem— just a continuation of the long, hard work of building a healthy civil society and the robust institutions that can steer it.

Turkey's Kurdish Buffer

Why Erdogan Is Ready to Work With the Kurds

Soner Cagaptay

If anything good comes out of the turmoil in Iraq, it will be improved ties between Turkey and the region's Kurds.

Until recently, they were bitter enemies. Ankara had never been able to stomach the idea of Kurdish self-government—in Iraq or Syria or Turkey—and it had generally refused to give in to Turkish Kurds' demands for cultural rights. Instead, it preferred to crack down. Meanwhile, the region's Kurds had never been able to stomach Iraqi, Syrian, or Turkish rule and, taking issue with Ankara's treatment of Kurds within Turkey's borders, threw their support behind the Kurdistan Workers' Party (PKK), a violent separatist movement in Turkey.

The Syrian civil war and developments in Iraq have started to change all that. These days, from Turkey's perspective, Kurdish autonomy doesn't look half bad. The portions of northern Iraq and Syria that are under Kurdish control are stable and peaceful—a perfect bulwark against threats such as the Islamic State of Iraq and al-Sham (ISIS). And that is why Turkey has been on good behavior with the Iraqi Kurds, is working on its relations with the Syrian Kurds, and might finally be breaking the impasse with the Kurds in

SONER CAGAPTAY is Beyer Family Fellow at the Washington Institute for Near East Policy and author of *Rise of Turkey: The Twenty First-Century's First Muslim Power*.

its own territory. It is a tall order, but the stars may be aligned in favor of a Turkish-Kurdish axis.

BACK TO IRAQ

Relations between Turkey and the Iraqi Kurds started improving just after the Iraq War, when Iraqi Kurds pivoted toward Ankara to counter Baghdad's centralizing pull. To the Kurds' dismay, post-Saddam Iraq remained an Arab country to the core; the power only shifted from Sunni Arabs to Shia Arabs. In those days, Iraqi Kurds started offering assistance to Turkey in its fight against the PKK and also opened markets in Iraqi Kurdistan to Turkish exports and companies. Turkey reciprocated, sending merchants, airlines, and consumer goods into the area. More recently, Iraqi Kurds opted to start selling their oil through Turkey, bypassing Baghdad and giving Ankara a huge gift in transit fees and tax revenue, as well as boosting Turkey's claim to be a regional energy hub.

ISIS' advances in Iraq—including a June 11 attack on the Turkish consulate in Mosul, during which the group took Turkish diplomats and security officials hostage—has added urgency to the drive to improve relations between Turkey and Iraqi Kurds. It also made Turkey go back on some clear redlines it had previously set for the Kurds; back in 2005, Turkey had threatened military action should they occupy Kirkuk, an oil-rich city in northern Iraq. Kirkuk's oil reserves would have given the Kurdish regional government independent income (it relies on Baghdad for financial transfers), which would have been a first step toward full sovereignty. But on June 12, when Kurdish forces moved to occupy Kirkuk, Ankara did not utter a word.

It now seems safe to say that if the Iraqi Kurdish regional government declared independence Ankara would be the first capital to recognize it. In today's Middle East, in other words, ISIS is a bigger threat to the Turks than Kurdish independence in Iraq.

SYRIAN SITUATION

Whereas Turkey's ties with the Iraqi Kurds have improved in recent years, Ankara's relations with the Syrian Kurds have remained rather bitter. This is because, unlike in the KRG where Iraqi Kurdish groups hold more sway than the Turkish PKK, the PKK is very popular among the Syrian Kurds. (Assad's father allowed the PKK to grow inside Syria to use the group as a proxy against Turkey.) When the group's Syrian branch, Party for Democratic Unity (PYD), which is not shy about its ties to the PKK, took control of Kurdish areas in northern Syria in July 2012, Ankara feared that it was witnessing the birth of a PKK-led state on its doorstep. In response, it stopped shipments of aid and supplies into the Kurdish enclaves.

As the war against Syrian President Bashar al-Assad heated up, though, Turkey saw an opportunity. Wishing to take advantage of all opposition factions in Syria, Turkey reached out to the PYD and invited the group's leader to Ankara. The PYD demurred, though. All along, the Kurds' strategy in the Syrian civil war has been simple: take over Kurdish areas and let the others fight among themselves. At times, the PYD has even collaborated with the Assad regime, for instance by allowing supplies to flow into regime-controlled enclaves. In return, Assad has not targeted PYD territory. It didn't make much sense, then, for the PYD to cooperate outright with Turkey.

But with the emergence of ISIS, the Syrian Kurds' calculations might be changing. The PYD and PKK have strong secular tendencies and oppose ISIS and its austere version of Islam. The PYD now controls three Kurdish exclaves in northern Syria, all of which are flanked by Turkey to the north and ISIS to the south. And unlike the Assad regime, ISIS has shown no inclination to trade favors with the Kurds. In other words, the Syrian Kurds' future could now be in Turkey's hands. It could allow more aid and supplies to flow to the Kurds to support their defensive lines against ISIS and, if the Syrian Kurds play nice, full military and security cooperation could be forthcoming.

Over time, Turkey believes, the Syrian Kurdish exclaves could become forward operating bases against ISIS—a friendly force that guards over 450 miles of Syria's 540-mile long Turkish border. The idea is appealing: the PYD is the only force, Assad regime included, that has been able to win any battle against ISIS in Syria. For instance, in March 2013, PYD fighters successfully pushed back an ISIS advance to take over Kobani, one of the three Kurdish exclaves in Syria.

TURKISH TROUBLE

Turkey cannot grow closer to Iraqi and Syrian Kurds without making peace with its own. After decades of battle, the PKK could still easily derail any rapprochement between Turkey and other Kurdish groups, especially the Syrian Kurds, by telling the PYD to reject Turkish offers. What is more, the PKK could launch attacks in Turkey if it feels that it is being left out of a potential deal between Turkey and the Iraqi Kurds.

Turkish Prime Minister Recep Tayyip Erdogan has a personal stake in this as well. He is facing a presidential election in August. In local elections in March, his party received 43 percent of the vote. The support of the pro-PKK Peace and Democracy Party, which won about 6.5 percent of the vote in March, could help him clinch the presidency.

Enter ongoing peace talks with the PKK. Through those negotiations, Turkey has granted the Kurds additional rights to use their own language in public, which had long been seen as a threat to Turkish nationalism. Kurdish language is now ubiquitous in universities and city governments in southeastern Turkey, where the Kurds dominate. More recently, on June 26, Erdogan declared a new reform package that promises amnesty for thousands of PKK fighters should negotiations with the PKK conclude successfully.

Erdogan will try to keep Turkish Kurds happy while building deeper security ties with the Iraqi and Syrian Kurds, which Turkey will guarantee de facto autonomy. This turn of events is rather ironic. Soon after Erdogan came to power in 2003, he launched a policy, called "strategic depth," which aimed to make Turkey a major power in the Middle East, with allies and influence across the region. A decade later, Ankara's only allies in the Middle East might just be the Kurds. Likewise, the Kurds' main ally might soon be Ankara. Working together, they will try to escape the old politics of the Middle East and stand alone as peaceful and stable success stories.

ISIS Enters Egypt

How Washington Must Respond

Khalil al-Anani

The Islamic State of Iraq and al-Sham (ISIS) has officially entered Egypt. On November 10, Ansar Beit al-Maqdis, a militant movement that operates out of the northern Sinai Peninsula, pledged allegiance to ISIS and its leader, Abu Bakr al-Baghdadi. The group, which emerged after the 2011 uprising that overthrew Egyptian President Hosni Mubarak, has already established itself as a formidable player in its own right. In recent months, it has staged devastating attacks on Egypt's police forces and claimed responsibility for a series of suicide attacks on military facilities in Cairo and the Sinai Peninsula.

The announcement was not a complete surprise, however, coming just weeks after Egyptian President Abel Fattah al-Sisi declared a state of emergency in the Sinai Peninsula and launched a bloody offensive against the group, which required an evacuation of Rafah that displaced approximately 10,000 people. Moreover, Ansar Beit al-Maqdis and ISIS are natural partners: They share not only a radical ideology but also barbaric tactics. Last August, Ansar Beit al-Maqdis decapitated four local men in northern Sinai after accusing them of being informants for Israel. But the decision to join ISIS marks the end of a bitter dispute within the militant movement's rank-and-file over whether to join the global group.

KHALIL AL-ANANI is an Adjunct Professor of Middle Eastern Studies at the Johns Hopkins School of Advanced International Studies (SAIS) and the author of the forthcoming book *Inside the Muslim Brotherhood: Religion, Identity and Politics.* Follow him on Twitter @Khalilalanani.

The split concerned two interlinked issues. The first was whether Ansar Beit al-Maqdis should join a global network or continue to operate independently. Some of the group's leaders argued—and failed to convince their peers—that focusing solely on Egypt would secure local support. The second was the choice between joining al Qaeda and ISIS. Whereas the group's veterans generally preferred the former, younger members pressed to join the latter.

Ansar Beit al-Maqdis' new ambitions provide yet another sign that Sisi's campaign of blind and brutal repression has backfired: Over the past few years, the militant group has grown only more appealing to disillusioned young Egyptians. And, in turn, it has expanded its objectives. In the months after Mubarak's ouster, the group focused mainly on staging attacks against targets in Israel and Sinai. In August 2011, it launched an assault on the southern Israeli city of Eilat, killing eight Israelis and five Egyptian soldiers. And throughout 2011 and 2012, the group frequently bombed the natural gas pipelines that run through Sinai to Israel and Jordan. It was not until after Sisi seized power, in July 2013, that the group moved into Egypt's heartland and started targeting government officials and security facilities. Now, according to a recent report, Ansar Beit al-Maqdis' attacks on greater Cairo have become as frequent as—and more deadly than—its assaults in Sinai.

Analysts now fear that the group may have sympathizers in the Egyptian military's ranks. Since Sisi's coup, a significant number of military officers has defected and joined radical groups. According to the Egyptian media, a devastating attack against the military checkpoint in Sinai last October, which killed 31 soldiers and injured many others, was planned and executed by two former army officers, Emad Abdel Halim and Hesham Ashmawy. There has also been speculation that a defected navy officer was involved in a recent Ansar Beit al-Maqdis assault on an Egyptian ship in the Mediterranean that left five navy officers injured and eight missing. And according to a recent *New York Times* report, Ansar Beit al-Maqdis is believed to be recruiting informants who know intimate details about the army's deployments. Such leaks could prove devastating, ushering a new era of insurgency that could haunt Egypt for years to come.

The new jihadist alliance is a disaster for Washington as well as Cairo. For one thing, it is proof positive that ISIS has been able to use its victories in Iraq and Syria to attract new followers and continued support outside the Levant—despite the fact that it is facing the fury of a U.S.-led air campaign. Egypt, moreover, home to such veteran jihadists as al Qaeda leader Ayman Al-Zawahiri (who despite his best efforts, has never been able to establish a foothold there), has become a full-fledged area of ISIS operations. For the group's leaders, Egypt plays a central role in its vision of an Islamic caliphate, not only because of the country's political and cultural stature in the Arab world, but also because of its borders with Israel. Further attacks on the Jewish state could help ISIS legitimize its operations and enhance its popularity among Egyptians.

Sisi, meanwhile, is losing touch with the country's moderate Muslims. The story of Ahmed al-Darawi, a 38-year-old rights activist who died last month fighting under the ISIS flag in Iraq, provides but a single well-reported example of a mainstream Egyptian turning violent. Al-Darawi, like many of his peers, grew disenchanted by the lack of reforms to state institutions in post-uprising Egypt, especially when it came to the Ministry of Interior, where he served as an officer before resigning to protest corruption. According to some estimates, ISIS currently has roughly 5,000 Egyptian fighters. Many are veteran jihadists who fought previously in Afghanistan and Bosnia during the 1980s and 1990s. And according to Egyptian officials, a number of them have already returned to lead operations against Sisi's regime.

The new allegiance thus further underscores how unstable Egypt remains. Through its clampdown on political dissent, Cairo has created a fertile ground for ISIS and groups like it, with the potential to recruit young people, Islamists, and moderates alike. Ansar Beit al-Maqdis is also capitalizing on Sisi's repressive policies in Sinai, which have alienated most of its population and allowed the group to drum up tribal support there.

The consequences of the alliance will be felt regionally as well. Even if ISIS is defeated in Iraq and Syria, a foothold in Egypt could provide access to safe havens in North and Sub-Saharan Africa, as well as in the Arab Peninsula. With dozens of supporters and sympathizers in Algeria, Libya, Mali, Morocco, Nigeria, and Tunisia, ISIS is poised to transform this massive area, drawing support from alienated citizens fed up with autocratic regimes. In addition, the new alliance could inspire other networks in these countries to join ISIS. Jihadist militias, such as Ansar al-Sharia in Libya and Boko Haram in Nigeria, are already appropriating ISIS' ideology and tactics to expand their own spheres of control.

All this further complicates U.S. President Barack Obama's efforts to renew congressional support for the allied military campaign against ISIS, raising further doubts about its effectiveness in the face of **diminishing** public support. U.S. military support for Egypt, which appears to have been largely ineffective in fighting terrorism, also stands at risk. New Apache helicopters and fighter jets, part of Washington's $1.3 billion annual aid package to Cairo, have failed to restore security in Sinai. In fact, Sisi's use of U.S. military equipment probably undermined his legitimacy, giving his counterterrorism campaign the appearance of U.S.-backed punishment.

Moving forward, the Obama administration will be tempted to give Sisi a blank check to fight Ansar Beit al-Maqdis and ISIS. But if Washington is to have any hope of succeeding in the larger fight against ISIS and its affiliates, the United States must ensure that any military support does not solidify autocratic rule or target innocents. It goes without saying that Sisi, like his fellow Arab autocrats, will derive his own benefit from the new alliance, allowing him to justify his despotic policies against political activists and dissenters. Yet recent events suggest that such an approach could backfire, leaving the United States and its allies to pick up the pieces.

ISIS' Next Prize

Will Libya Join the Terrorist Group's Caliphate?

Geoffrey Howard

The Islamic State of Iraq and al-Sham is no longer just an Iraq and Syria problem. For months now, ISIS (or groups affiliated with it) has been pushing into Libya as well. The country has long been vulnerable; the vacuum created by the deepening political crisis and collapse of state institutions is an attractive arena for terrorist groups. Further, control of Libya could potentially bring access to substantial revenues through well-established smuggling networks that deal in oil, stolen cars, contraband goods, and weapons.

It should perhaps not have been surprising, then, when Libyan militants claimed Derna, in the country's lawless northeast, as an ISIS province in late 2014. ISIS leader Abu Bakr al-Baghdadi welcomed the declaration and sent an emir to lead operations in the town. He also announced the creation of three other ISIS provinces in the country: Barqa in the east, Tripoli in the west, and Fezzan in the south. More recently, groups linked to ISIS have claimed responsibility for a number of attacks, including in Tripoli, Sirte, and Gubba, and they have seized urban centers, including Nawfaliyah and parts of Sirte. In early February, moreover, an ISIS-allied group beheaded 21 Egyptian Coptic Christians in Libya, demonstrating the seriousness of ISIS' intentions.

Yet it is easy to overstate ISIS' influence in Libya. Libya is home to a broad range of militant groups, and the vast majority of violent

---

GEOFFREY HOWARD is Control Risks' lead Libya analyst.

attacks in the country are carried out by domestic groups—including tribes, ethnic minorities, and members of the security forces and militias—who are motivated by more local grievances tied to the rule of Muammar al-Qaddafi (he encouraged rivalry between factions), the 2011 uprising (which was itself a series of localized pockets of resistance rather than a nationwide movement), and subsequent fighting for control of the country (which has deepened the old divisions).

Indeed, Libya's post-uprising political dynamics may actually hinder ISIS more than any airstrikes. Libya is highly fragmented. Multiple competing power centers front their own armed groups and political structures, each with varying degrees of affiliation to each other and to the country's two rival governments. They also have conflicting demands and expectations, and rivalries going back decades. Among these groups, however, sectarian tensions are not as heightened as they are in Iraq and Syria (over 95 percent of the population is Sunni). Moreover, Libya's local political actors are stronger and less likely to present ISIS with any opportunities to foment further divisions and create strongholds.

It will be hard for ISIS to navigate the maze of competing local, ethnic, tribal, ideological, and political groups. Most all of them are ultimately self-serving and self-interested, and ISIS' advance would threaten their own political and economic agendas. Armed groups already compete fiercely for control of the lucrative smuggling networks that traverse the region. ISIS' attempts to take a piece of the pie for itself would not go over well, nor would any efforts to gain control over oil and gas infrastructure. At present, these groups are likely able to resist ISIS' attempts to gain control over these strategic interests. In addition, greater ISIS presence in Libya could even provide a common enemy for the armed groups, bringing them together—at least as long as the threat remains.

Even if ISIS were able to take over some of Libya's prize oil and gas infrastructure, the group would most likely struggle to make much money from it; oil output has already fallen to 350,000 barrels per day, down from total capacity export levels of around

1.6 million, a figure nearly reached in 2013 following a strong resurgence in the hydrocarbons sector immediately after the 2011 uprising. Hydrocarbon assets are generally located in inaccessible areas of the desert, with refining capabilities in large facilities far away on the coast. To turn a profit, then, ISIS would have to get control of the oilfields, the pipelines, and the export terminals. It would also face the extremely difficult task of organizing illicit exports. Although ISIS may be able to conduct low-level oil smuggling, talk of Libya as a potential gold mine—including claims from a number of Libyan ministers and officials in the Gulf that Libya could bankroll ISIS—may be premature.

ISIS' strength in Libya has so far been untested and its initial spread has been relatively easy; predisposed militants willingly latched on to the group's brand to gain notoriety. But ISIS' successes have so far been concentrated amongst Libyan militants in areas that already have a history of Islamist radicalism, such as Sirte, Derna, and Benghazi. The momentum may be difficult to sustain. ISIS does not enjoy broad support in Libya, and efforts to maintain recruitment levels will be complicated by Libya's small population, the lack of serious sectarian divisions between Sunni and Shia, and the potential backlash against barbarous acts carried out in the name of ISIS.

At the same time, Libya is undoubtedly exposed; should the chronic political crisis reach a tipping point, spiraling levels of violence could provide ISIS-affiliated groups with greater space to operate, filling the vacuum left by defunct institutions and a fragmented society. The prolonged political crisis is already causing splits within Libya's two main political blocs, and hard-line factions within both are agitating for more extreme action. ISIS may find willing recruits among these fringe radicals, as well as among foreign fighters from al Qaeda in the Islamic Maghreb, which has been struggling to remain relevant.

Still, an ISIS stronghold in Libya is hardly a fait accompli. Further attacks by ISIS-affiliated groups are almost certain, but the group will face more hurdles in building a caliphate than a cursory narrative about Libya's impending state collapse suggests.

Crime and Punishment in Jordan

The Killing of Moath al-Kasasbeh and the Future of the War Against ISIS

David Schenker

T he Islamic State of Iraq and al-Sham's horrific video of operatives burning alive the captured Jordanian pilot Moath al-Kasasbeh shocked the world. King Abdullah, who was visiting Washington when the video was released, vowed to avenge Kasasbeh's death and promptly returned to Jordan. Even before he landed, two prominent al Qaeda prisoners with ties to ISIS on death row in the kingdom were hanged.

Jordanians greeted Abdullah's arrival—and the news of the two executions—with jubilation. But the kingdom's next moves against ISIS remain unclear. Jordanians want revenge, yet until now the kingdom's involvement in the U.S.-led air campaign against the terrorist group has been deeply unpopular at home. Indeed, until Kasasbeh's death, the trending Twitter hashtag in Jordan was #ThisIsNotOurWar.

If the past is precedent, Kasasbeh's death at the hands of ISIS could signal a change—at least temporarily—in Jordanian popular

DAVID SCHENKER is director of the Program on Arab Politics at the Washington Institute for Near East Policy. From 2002 to 2006, he served as Levant Director in the Office of the Secretary of Defense.

attitudes toward the war and presage a more robust role for the kingdom in military operations.

For the past six months, opposition to the war in Jordan was broad-based, including both secular and Islamist residents. The Jordanian Muslim Brotherhood condemned participation in the coalition as a violation of the country's constitution and "a campaign against Islam." Meanwhile, some secular Jordanians worried that the kingdom's role in the air war would provoke ISIS retaliation. Still others—such as the prominent columnist Lamis Andoni—contended that Jordan had been blackmailed by the United States, the kingdom's leading donor, into participating. The campaign, she wrote on December 30, represented a "complete subordination to Washington's policies and wishes."

For most Jordanians, though, opposition to the anti-ISIS coalition seemed to be driven by dynamics in Syria, where, since 2011, the nominally Shia Alawite regime of President Bashar al-Assad has killed 200,000 people, mostly Sunnis. In this context, many Jordanians saw the Sunni ISIS as an effective counterforce to Assad. Not surprisingly, according to a poll published in September by the Center for Strategic Studies at the University of Jordan, only 62 percent of Jordanians considered ISIS to be a terrorist organization.

Even before Kasasbeh's capture by ISIS in Syria last year, burgeoning opposition to Jordan's participation in the war was a growing headache for the palace. It became worse after. Although the Jordanian military—known at home as the Arab Army—remained extremely popular, Jordanian leaders were coming under increasing criticism for allowing the country to serve as the base of coalition air operations. The pilot's father, Safi Yousef al Kasasbeh, emerged as a prominent critic of the war and of the ineffectual palace efforts to negotiate or otherwise secure his son's release.

If the 2005 Amman hotel bombings—the worst in Jordanian history—are any indication, Kasasbeh's execution could shift local public opinion. Prior to the November 2005 attack on three downtown hotels that killed 60 and wounded 115, 61 percent of

Jordanians reported that they viewed Osama bin Laden favorably. In polling after the bombing, which was perpetrated by al Qaeda's Iraq affiliate, support for bin Laden plummeted to 24 percent. And five years later, confidence in the al Qaeda leader bottomed out at just 13 percent.

To be sure, much has changed since 2005. A decade ago, for example, the region wasn't engulfed in a Sunni-Shia conflict and Jordan wasn't witnessing the exponential growth of Salafism. To wit, even after Kasasbeh, some Jordanian Islamist leaders apparently still can't bring themselves to condemn ISIS. Complicating matters, an estimated 2,500 Jordanians are currently fighting jihad in Syria—an occurrence so common that just last week, it barely made local headlines that the son of a sitting parliamentarian was killed fighting for Jebhat al-Nusra in Aleppo.

Nevertheless, the Kasasbeh outrage and the 2005 bombing in Amman have similar implications for Jordanian policy. At a minimum, like 2005, this incident will convince many Jordanians that the kingdom is in ISIS' crosshairs, limiting, at least temporarily, opposition to membership in the U.S.-led coalition. Accordingly, Jordanians will be more amenable to proactive kinetic operations. Not surprisingly, given current popular sentiment, Abdullah's latest calls for a "relentless" and "harsh" war against ISIS in Syria have been well received. In the coming days and weeks, it seems likely that Jordan will increase the frequency and ferocity of its air operations—and perhaps even deploy special forces—to target ISIS in Syria.

Although an immediate robust Jordanian military response is appropriate, however, it's not at all certain that the kingdom will keep up the tempo of operations after the fury over Kasasbeh dissipates. By regional standards, the Jordanian military is impressive, consistently demonstrating a high level of commitment and courage. However, for Jordan—indeed, for any military—a surge of operations almost necessarily means an increase in casualties.

Six months into the air war, Jordan has lost two F-16s and one pilot, in addition to dozens of ground forces wounded and killed along the frontier with Syria. Jordan is already at the so-called tip of the spear of the campaign, but the prospect of increased casualties—who will almost certainly hail from the country's tribes, which constitute the backbone of the military and the leading supporters of the monarchy—holds little appeal for the king.

Perhaps the abiding tribal concept of *thar* (revenge) will mitigate future backlash against the palace for losses sustained in the fight against ISIS. Although Jordan is not a democracy, public sentiment matters, particularly in these difficult times. And the lesson of the Kasasbeh hostage ordeal is that the kingdom is quite sensitive to military casualties. Here, though, history is key. The rage in the kingdom following the 2005 bombings persisted for a year—and coincided with increased Jordanian military and intelligence cooperation with the United States on al Qaeda, as well as draconian security measures on the home front. On both accounts, there was little popular protest.

For the time being, with the overwhelming support of the population, Abdullah will extract revenge on ISIS in Syria. He will also have a freer hand to pursue a more comprehensive crackdown on ISIS supporters at home. Over time, however, concerns about force preservation may ultimately compel the kingdom to dial back its own expanded military efforts in Syria. Committed to the coalition, Jordan will remain the base of anti-ISIS air operations and a training facility for anti-Assad Syrian rebels for the foreseeable future. But Jordan is unlikely to become a regional Sparta—as *The Washington Post* recently described the United Arab Emirates—anytime soon. ISIS poses a clear and present danger to Jordan's stability, but so does popular discontent.

This is What Détente Looks Like

The United States and Iran Join Forces Against ISIS

Mohsen Milani

I t is no particular surprise that U.S. President Barack Obama is on the verge of turning over a new leaf with Iran. After all, over the course of his presidency, Obama has repeatedly emphasized that he would like the United States and Iran to overcome their 35 years of estrangement. What is surprising, however, is how rapprochement has come about—not through negotiations over the fate of Tehran's nuclear program, but as a result of the battle against ISIS.

Tehran and Washington find themselves on the same side in the fight against the Islamic State of Iraq and al-Sham (ISIS), also called the Islamic State (IS), and there are already signs that they have been cooperating against the extremist group's advance through Iraq. Although there is no guarantee that this will last for the duration of the war, such cooperation is clearly a positive step.

The United States and Iran both view ISIS as a significant threat to their own interests. An ISIS stronghold near the Iranian border would be a profound and immediate security threat to Tehran. For one, the Sunni jihadists of ISIS are openly disdainful of

MOHSEN MILANI is Professor of Politics and the Executive Director of the Center for Strategic and Diplomatic Studies at the University of South Florida. Follow him on Twitter @mohsenmilani.

the Shia faith, the sect of Islam that the overwhelming majority of Iranians and the majority of Iraqis adhere to. The group is already in a sectarian war in Syria and Iraq, and Tehran must assume that it eventually plans on turning its attention to Iran.

Washington, for its part, has also concluded that ISIS poses a significant threat. If ISIS manages to create a safe haven in Iraq, it could use the territory to plan operations against the West, undermine Western allies in the region, and endanger oil shipments in the Persian Gulf. In the meantime, the group's war against the Iraqi state also poses a danger to U.S. interests. Over the past decade, Washington has paid a high price in blood and treasure to create a stable and relatively friendly Iraq. The collapse of that state would be a humiliating defeat.

Although the United States and Iran have different visions for the future of Iraq, they share three major strategic goals there: protecting Iraq's territorial integrity; preventing a sectarian civil war that could easily metastasize into the entire region; and defeating ISIS. There is also a precedent of tactical cooperation in Iraq between Tehran and Washington: In 2001, the two cooperated to dislodge the Taliban from Afghanistan.

Obama has pledged not to tolerate the establishment of a terrorist state in Iraq and has already ordered limited air strikes against ISIS to protect U.S. personnel and facilities in Iraq and provide humanitarian relief to that country's desperate Yezidi minority. Tehran has given unambiguous signals that it approves of Obama's limited military mission. Iranian President Hassan Rouhani and a host of other officials have publicly expressed willingness to collaborate with the United States to defeat ISIS. It is unlikely that Tehran will offer tactical assistance to the United States on the battlefield, of course, but it is likely to welcome continued U.S. air strikes and might even quietly applaud the reintroduction of U.S. ground troops to Iraq.

But Obama has also declared, correctly, that there can't be a U.S. military solution for Iraq's problems until its political problems—above all, its central government's tendency toward exclusivism—have been addressed. This is where Iran, which has maintained very close ties with the Shia parties that are dominant in Baghdad, has taken the lead. Washington has greeted the arrival of Iraq's new prime minister, Haider al-Abadi. Abadi's predecessor, Nouri al-Maliki, only stepped down after Iran (and Ayatollah Ali Sistani, Iraq's leading Shia cleric) firmly pushed him to go. Tehran initially expressed its desire for Maliki to leave office in private. But when he still showed no signs of exiting, Ali Shamkhani, Secretary of Iran's Supreme National Security Council, issued a public declaration congratulating Abadi for being named to form a new government. Tehran also mobilized Iraqi Shia groups as well as Shia militias to support Abadi. Washington was reduced to being an observer in much of this process, but it welcomed the outcome.

The cooperation between Tehran and Washington in Iraq has been productive so far, but it is also fragile. There are three factors that could easily derail it. The first is a dispute over the composition of the new Iraqi government. Iran recognized that Maliki had become too polarizing and authoritarian a figure, but that does not mean that it has otherwise revised its strategy that Iraq's Shia community should dominate Iraqi politics, or changed its view that Sunni groups need to learn to accept Shia rule. As I wrote in an earlier article for *Foreign Affairs*, this is both a matter of principle (Shias comprise a comfortable majority of the Iraqi population) and pragmatism (Tehran believes that the Sunnis are less likely than the Shias and Kurds to be interested in building close ties with Iran).

Washington, by contrast, believes that Iraq's Shia community should wield less power than it naturally would under strict proportionality according to population. In part, this may be because of pressure from Sunni governments in the region, including Saudi Arabia. But the United States also believes that some of Iraq's Shia groups are more interested in acquiring a monopoly over national power than wielding power in a responsible fashion.

The second factor that could stall U.S.–Iranian cooperation is the prospect of an independent Kurdistan. Under Maliki, the relationship between Baghdad and the Kurdish regional capital of Erbil, became increasingly hostile. After the northern Iraqi city of Mosul fell to ISIS in June, the Kurds decided to seize the opportunity to make a bid for greater sovereignty. They quickly captured Kirkuk, a contested and energy-rich city in northern Iraq, and continued with their controversial policy to sell oil without Baghdad's approval. They also stated their intention to hold a referendum on Kurdish independence.

All of these developments alarmed Tehran, which has generally maintained good relations with the Kurds, but has drawn a red line regarding Kurdish independence. The recent decision by Western countries to provide weapons directly to Kurdish militias has increased Tehran's anxieties. Although Iran has developed close political and economic ties with Iraq's Kurds and has even pledged to support them in their war against ISIS, Tehran also understands that independence for Iraqi Kurds could easily incite Iran's own ethnic minorities to demand independence and undermine the country's territorial integrity. Tehran is very aware of a recent precedent: After World War II, an independent government was fleetingly established in Mahabad, in Iranian Kurdistan, although the Soviet-backed movement was soon crushed by Iran's central government. Iranian policymakers also know that, although the United States officially opposes Kurdish independence, the Kurds have powerful friends in Washington who seek to change that policy.

Finally, U.S.–Iranian cooperation can always falter because of the many constituencies in both countries that are ideologically opposed to any bilateral cooperation between the two states. In Washington, many blame Iran for encouraging sectarianism in Iraq, and correctly point out that Iran trained and funded the Shia militias that killed U.S. troops after the initial invasion of Iraq. They consider Iran to be the source of Iraq's problems and sincerely, if unrealistically, seek to exclude it from any future security architecture of the country. For example, General James L. Jones, Obama's former National Security Advisor, recently proposed convening a U.S.-sponsored strategic conference about Iraq. All regional players are to be invited to the conference, except Iran.

Similarly, many members of the security forces in Tehran reject cooperation with the United States. They believe that Washington is the source of instability in Iraq; some even blame the United States for the existence of ISIS, based on the conspiratorial belief that the United States helped finance the group so that it would fight against the Tehran-backed Assad regime in Syria. For Iran's most devout Islamist ideologues, the United States can never be trusted beyond very short-term tactical cooperation.

Despite these difficulties, cooperation between Washington and Tehran is likely to deepen, rather than ebb, in the weeks ahead. ISIS is a clear transnational threat that demands a transnational solution. Iran has considerable experience fighting against ISIS in Syria and Lebanon and can offer much assistance to those who seek to eradicate the threat posed by the militant group. Indeed, the fight against ISIS may even produce the previously unthinkable: cooperation between Iran and Saudi Arabia, two countries that have more or less fought an open proxy war for the past several years in Iraq, Lebanon, and Syria. Now, both countries are threatened by ISIS, which explains why Saudi Arabia openly welcomed Abadi's nomination to become prime minister.

Two weeks ago, Alaeddin Boroujerdi, chairman of the Iranian parliament's Foreign Policy and National Security Committee, correctly stated that Iran, Saudi Arabia, and the United States are the key players in Iraq. If Washington and Tehran manage to cooperate to stabilize in Iraq, it would not only be good news for the Iraqis—it could also pave the way for a final agreement in the ongoing nuclear negotiations. In that sense, the two countries would have truly achieved significant rapprochement, if not in the way that many observers originally anticipated.

ISIS Goes to Asia

Extremism in the Middle East Isn't Only Spreading West

Joseph Chinyong Liow

A s the United States sought in recent weeks to assemble an international coalition to combat the Islamic State of Iraq and al-Sham (ISIS, also known as the Islamic State), it looked mostly to the Middle East and Europe, regions that it said face a direct threat from the militant Islamist group. But other parts of the world are just as anxious about ISIS—above all, Southeast Asia. The governments of that region have not publicized their concerns very loudly, but they are acutely aware that ISIS is a menace. Their top concern is that its extremist ideology will prove attractive to the region's many Muslims, lure some of them to the Middle East to fight as part of the group, and ultimately be imported back to the region when these militants return home.

There is a clear precedent for this scenario. During the 1980s, many young Muslims from Southeast Asia went to Pakistan to support the Afghan mujahideen's so-called jihad against Soviet occupation. Many of these recruits subsequently stayed in the region, mingling with like-minded Muslims from all around and gaining exposure to al Qaeda's militant ideology. Many eventually returned to Southeast Asia to form extremist groups of their own, including

JOSEPH CHINYONG LIOW is Senior Fellow and Lee Kuan Yew Chair in Southeast Asian Studies at the Brookings Institution and Professor and Associate Dean at the S.Rajaratnam School of International Studies, Nanyang Technological University.

the notorious al Qaeda–linked organization Jemaah Islamiyah that was responsible for several high-profile terrorist attacks in the region over the last 15 years. With evidence now surfacing of Southeast Asians among the ranks of ISIS casualties, it's only natural that governments in the region are feeling a sense of déjà vu.

RADICAL CHIC

Singapore has already revealed that several of its nationals have made their way to the Middle East to battle with ISIS, and the Philippine government has suggested that local ISIS sympathizers are attempting to recruit from among the Bangsamoro populations in the country's southern islands. But the greatest concern comes from Indonesia and Malaysia. Indonesia, the world's most populous Muslim country, has already confirmed that more than 50 of its citizens are currently fighting in Syria and Iraq; Malaysia has suggested that between 30 and 40 Malaysians are doing the same. In both cases, the actual numbers could be much higher if we consider those who may have traveled to the conflict zones from other destinations. Indonesian authorities have already noted that several of their nationals have been killed fighting for ISIS in Syria. On May 26, a Malaysian suicide bomber killed himself in an ISIS attack in Iraq. Another Malaysian fighter who died fighting for ISIS in Syria several months later has been celebrated as a martyr by leaders of the Pan-Malaysian Islamic Party, the same party that had earlier dismissed him after he departed for Syria. Intriguingly, three Malaysian women were also alleged to have left for Syria to wage a "sexual jihad" (*jihad al-nikah*), offering their bodies to ISIS fighters to "boost their morale."

ISIS' reach in Southeast Asia is based on several factors. First, certain devout Muslims feel a theological affinity for the militant group. They see parallels between ISIS' mission and prophecies in Islamic holy texts of the eventual creation of a *Khilafah Minhaj Nebuwwah* ("end-times caliphate") following the fall of dictators in the Arabian Peninsula; they are also reminded of the apocalyptic struggle that is said to be fated between the forces of Imam Mahdi, an Islamic messiah figure who is supposed to fight under a black flag, and those of the Dajjal, or Antichrist. Anecdotal evidence suggests that this millenarian perspective is growing in Indonesia and Malaysia with radical clerics such as Aman Abdurrahman, who, though in jail, are expanding their reach through the Internet and radical tracts—including a book titled *Strategi Dua Lengan* (*Two-Armed Strategy*)—increasingly finding their way into Indonesian translation.

Another reason for ISIS' appeal is its sectarianism. The ISIS challenge is seen in some quarters as an extension of the Sunni-Shiite schism. To wit: The group's struggle against Bashar al-Assad's Alawite regime is considered legitimate in fundamentalist Sunni-Salafi circles. In much the same way, ISIS militancy in Iraq is seen as a consequence of Sunni grievance against the Shiite-led government of Nouri al-Maliki. This support needs to be understood in the context of Southeast Asia's own problems with sectarianism: Shiite Islam is banned in Malaysia and is not widely accepted in Indonesia.

Finally, the question of the recruitment of Southeast Asians into ISIS cannot be divorced from the larger context of the humanitarian crisis in Syria. The universal sympathy for the Syrian people among Southeast Asia's sizable Muslim populations has undoubtedly prompted a large number of humanitarian missions to depart for the conflict zone. Many members of these missions may well have set off with noble intentions. But once they arrive in territory held by ISIS, it is not difficult to imagine how they would be exposed to ISIS indoctrination and recruitment.

FALSE ANALOGY

In many ways, Southeast Asia seems to be seeing a repeat of its experience with Afghanistan in the 1980s and 1990s. The most familiar aspect is ISIS' recruiting efforts, mostly undertaken by Southeast Asian sympathizers rather than ISIS leaders based in the Middle East. In 2012, ISIS' appeal started to grow among Indonesian and Malaysian civil society groups that had mobilized in response to Syria's humanitarian crisis by creating local awareness and fundraising. Within a year, several Islamic preachers in Indonesia had pledged allegiance to ISIS' caliphate, and about half a dozen graduates from Indonesia's Ngruki Islamic boarding school, previously a hotbed of Jemaah Islamiyah membership ideology and recruitment, are believed to have left to join the jihad in Syria (often with funding from Jemaah Islamiyah and other affiliated extremist groups). ISIS has also been actively recruiting in Malaysia through Islamic study groups known as *usrah*. In turn, those Malaysian recruits are believed to have attempted to recruit from Singapore. It is still not yet known exactly how successful these recruiting efforts have been. But it is clear that ISIS has been able to promote its jihad through sympathizers plugged into the region's local Islamic communities and networks, just as Afghan militants did in earlier decades.

But there are also significant differences between the present-day jihad and the earlier one in Afghanistan against the Soviet Union. While the Afghan mujahideen's struggle was widely embraced, ISIS has proven extremely divisive in Southeast Asia, even among extremist groups, some of which have rejected and virulently condemned the organization. Jemaah Islamiyah, for one, has accused ISIS of being *takfir* (Muslims who pass judgment on fellow Muslims of being un-Islamic) and dismissed its members as *khawarij* (extremists). Other groups, such as the conservative Majelis Mujahidin Indonesia (Indonesian Mujahideen Council), have cast doubt on ISIS' religious credentials, proclaiming that it is an organization and not a caliphate and hence has no legitimate claim to the loyalty of Muslims. Furthermore, they have also argued that ISIS' process for appointing Abu Bakr al-Baghdadi as caliph was in violation of Islamic law, as it did not take place before a religious council that represents the entire Islamic community. As the terrorism expert Sidney Jones has rightly pointed out, the existence of this divergence of opinion on ISIS speaks to a split within Indonesia's extremist community between those who support ISIS and others who remain loyal to al Qaeda and the al Nusra Front.

Unsurprisingly, the other major difference from the days of the jihad in Afghanistan is ISIS' use of social media. ISIS has consistently used Twitter and Facebook to amplify its message and broaden its reach. Also, the fact that authorities in Indonesia have been reluctant to shut down radical websites that carry ISIS propaganda, such as al-Mustaqbal.net, despite already imposing a ban on the group's jihadist teachings (likely because of a misplaced concern for its religious credibility in the eyes of the vocal radical Islamist community), has only enhanced its visibility in the region.

KEEP CALM AND CARRY ON

Without downplaying the ISIS threat to Southeast Asia, there are nevertheless limits to the effectiveness of its recruitment in the region. Despite huge investments from Arab governments, particularly Saudi Arabia, in Islamic education across Southeast Asia over the past three decades, the lingua francas of the region's Muslim communities remain Malay and Indonesian, not Arabic. The vast majority of Muslims from the region are insufficiently literate in Arabic to even appreciate ISIS' propaganda without translation, much less fully integrate with ISIS fighters in Iraq and Syria. In Afghanistan during the 1980s and 1990s, this problem was in part surmounted by the creation of dedicated training camps for Southeast Asians; although the situation may change, this does not seem to be the case in Syria or Iraq at the moment, where Southeast Asian recruits are thrown onto the front lines with everyone else. Second, Muslims in Indonesia and Malaysia enjoy social and economic conditions far better than those of their coreligionists in the Levant (or even in Europe, where there is a palpable sense of alienation and marginalization among Muslim immigrant populations). By and large, Southeast Asians simply have fewer incentives to travel to Syria or Iraq.

Finally, unlike the immediate aftermath of the Afghan conflict in the 1990s, terrorist recruitment in Southeast Asia today has lost the tactical advantage of surprise. With regional security and intelligence agencies alert to the potential threat emanating from Iraq and Syria—thanks precisely to the lessons they learned from the 1990s—conditions are considerably more difficult for the kind of clandestine recruitment that went on two decades ago. Two other factors are instructive in this regard. First, whatever its shortcomings, the Indonesian state today is not nearly as weak as it was in the late 1990s, when radical groups flourished after the fall of former President Suharto. Second, the apparent resolution of the long-standing conflict in the Philippines between the government and the Moro Islamic Liberation Front has potentially opened the way for cooperation on counterterrorism.

That said, it's understandable that the governments of the region are concerned that ISIS might spawn a new generation of jihadist leaders, fighters, and ideologues in the region. Afghanistan still casts a long shadow over discussions in Southeast Asia—and with good reason. But regional policymakers would be well advised to appreciate not only the similarities between the former challenge and the present-day conflict but also the very significant differences.

They're Coming

Measuring the Threat from Returning Jihadists

Jytte Klausen

I n an interview with the Washington Post in May, FBI Director
James B. Comey, who also served as President George W. Bush's
deputy attorney general, compared the wave of militants pouring
into Syria and Iraq to the rush to join Osama bin Laden in Afghanistan as the Taliban swept that country. "We see Syria as that, but an
order of magnitude worse in a couple of respects," he said. "Far more
people going there. Far easier to travel to and back from."

But not everybody agrees that the United States should be
alarmed. Writing in the New Yorker last month, the journalist
Steve Coll pointed to "some terrorism specialists," who argue that
Islamic State of Iraq and al-Sham (ISIS) is fighting a sectarian war
and is more concerned with killing other Muslims than Westerners; that it "has shown no intent to launch attacks in the West, or
any ability to do so." In a widely cited article in the American Political Science Review, Thomas Hegghammer, a senior research fellow at the Norwegian Defense Establishment, argued that there is
an essential philosophical difference between those who carry out
attacks at home and those who go abroad to fight on behalf of al
Qaeda and its affiliates. Many of the Westerners who have gone to
Syria and Iraq, he wrote, are unlikely to want to attack targets at
home.

JYTTE KLAUSEN is Lawrence A. Wien Professor of International Cooperation
at Brandeis University.

Yet fighters returning from Syria have already attempted to carry out violent attacks in the West, and, in one instance, they succeeded. In October 2013, the London Metropolitan Police stopped a car traveling near the Tower of London carrying two men who were reportedly on their way to execute an attack. The two men, both London residents but not British citizens, had recently returned from Syria. In March this year, the French police unraveled a terrorist cell in Nice that was allegedly planning to use improvised explosive devices on the French Riviera. The perpetrators had also recently returned from Syria and were linked to a cell that was held responsible for an attack on a Paris kosher shop in September 2012. Then, at the end of May, Mehdi Nemmouche, a French citizen linked to a militant group known as Forsane Alizza (Knights of Pride), killed three people in front of the Jewish museum in Brussels. He also apparently took part in holding a group of journalists hostage in Syria between July 2013 and December 2013. In late July this year, the Norwegian government put the country on alert that four terrorists from ISIS were on their way to carry out a bombing in the country. The plan, it seems, was for the terrorists to kidnap a family, record themselves decapitating its members, and then post the video to YouTube. And finally, this week, the Australian police carried out the largest counterterrorism operation in the country's history against an ISIS-linked group based in Sydney. The group allegedly planned to carry out random beheadings of one or more pedestrians taken off the street.

This doesn't sound like a group of people who has no interest in attacking on Western soil.

BY THE NUMBERS

According to official estimates, about 3,000 Westerners have joined ISIS or Jabhat al-Nusra, the al Qaeda–affiliated group in Syria. In addition, hundreds of women from Europe and Australia (and a few Americans) have followed the men, marrying them online before they leave home or linking up with fighters after they arrive for training. They are already pushing against traditional jihadist gender boundaries by setting up female-only fighter groups and taking a prominent role on social media networks—including posting pictures of themselves with mutilated corpses. They could very well end up becoming violent themselves. If allowed back into their Western countries of origin, how many of these fighters— both the men and women—pose a serious threat to the West?

Here, historical data may provide a baseline estimate. For some years, I have worked with my students to track Westerners who have committed terrorist acts on behalf of al Qaeda and other jihadist groups in its mold. Between 2012 and May 2014, we identified—by name or fighter alias—600 who have left to fight in Syria and Iraq since June 2014. We also identified about 900 individuals who, between 1993 and until about 2012, fought in previous jihadist insurgencies or attempted to link up with terrorist groups and training camps abroad associated with al Qaeda, not including the jihadist groups in Syria and Iraq. Many of these veteran fighters fought in multiple insurgencies. Some of them are now back at work in Syria or Iraq, or have died fighting there. That makes for a data set of nearly 1,500 Western foreign fighters about whom we have basic demographic information, such as age and national and ethnic origin. We know which insurgency they participated in, and what they did after that.

The data show that, in fact, we should be very afraid of the "backflow" from Syria and Iraq. The experience of fighting in a foreign conflict zone, or receiving military-style training from a terrorist organization abroad, often primes Western militants to perpetrate a violent attack at home.

By our count, there have been approximately 279 violent terrorist plots on Western soil since 1993 that were unrelated to the ongoing mobilization in Syria and Iraq. (Here, "plot" might more accurately be described as an arrest related to plans or attempts to do something illegal related to terrorism.) Of the 279 plots, 114 (or 41 percent) included foreign fighters. We identified 275 foreign fighters overall who participated in these plots. Taking a baseline number of nearly 900 foreign fighters (all pre-Syria), in other words, approximately one-in-three Western fighters or veterans of training camps participated in a violent domestic plot. They also helped in fundraising, recruitment, and other schemes, but non-violent activities are not included in this risk assessment.

Of course, producing clean metrics is tricky. "Doing something" abroad and at home are closely related events, and the sequence does not necessarily go "training abroad and then violent action at home." (Of the 275 identified participants, 235, about 85 percent, participated in a Western plot after returning.) On occasion, perpetrators became foreign fighters after attempting violence in the West. In those cases, they were often fleeing to join a terrorist group abroad to avoid presenting themselves in court for trial. Others launched attacks after going abroad and failing to obtain sponsorship from an al Qaeda affiliate. Tarek Mehanna, a pudgy pharmacy student from Sudbury, Massachusetts, made no less than three unsuccessful attempts to join an al Qaeda affiliate abroad. After one of his unsuccessful trips, he and his friends played with the idea of shooting up a local mall.

We can drill down still further to look at so-called homegrown conspiracies following 9/11 that have posed a significant risk of large-scale civilian casualties—for example, the Boston Marathon Bombings, the failed 2009 plot by three school friends from Queens to bomb the New York City subway, and Faisal Shahzad's failed 2010 Times Square car bomb. We identified 24 such extremely violent plots on Western soil. Of these, 79 percent—four out of five—involved returning foreign fighters or individuals who had received training abroad. Of all returning foreign fighters, about one in 12 attempted something along these lines.

In short, not all Westerners return home from jihad abroad to take part in a violent attack. But many do, and they tend to become involved with extremely dangerous plans. Of course, alarming as these numbers are, the ratio of disrupted violent incidents to actualized ones is high—about four-to-one—and has increased since the early years of homegrown terrorism following the 9/11 attacks. The odds of disruption for the plots that posed a significant risk of mass casualties are about 50–50.

ATTACK-READY

Assuming that past behavior contains some insights into future behavior, the historical data can help policymakers assess the risk posed to domestic safety by Western returnees from the battle in Syria and Iraq. Combat zone death rates are high among the Western volunteers in Syria and Iraq, about one-in-three, by our count. Generally, insurgent casualty rates are high, but the Westerners are also often used as suicide bombers. (As one former ISIS fighter put it: "I saw many foreign recruits who were put in the suicide squads not because they were 'great and God wanted it' as [ISIS] commanders praised them in front of us, but basically because they were useless for ISIS, they spoke no Arabic, they weren't good fighters and had no professional skills.") Accepting the estimate that there are (or have been) about 3,000 Western fighters in the theater, we would expect that about a thousand will die. Of those who don't, most return home or travel to another Western country. Using the one-in-three ratio of returnees from previous conflicts who have come back to do something violent, we would expect over 600 returning fighters from Syria and Iraq to attempt to carry out a violent attack in a Western country within the next few years. This number does not include the essentially unknowable risk stemming from the women who have become radicalized during the time spent with their husbands in Iraq and Syria.

This is not to say that the current wave of jihadists is the same as previous waves. First, the demographics of Westerners in Syria and Iraq today are very different from those in previous jihadist insurgencies. For one, Western fighters in Syria are generally younger (with a mean age of 24) than in previous conflicts. In Bosnia, the average age was 30. In Pakistan and Afghanistan, before and after 9/11, the average was around 27. In the first jihadist insurgency in Iraq (2004–07), the fighters were nearly 28 years old. Recruitment through social media is often held responsible for the age shift, but ISIS has also deliberately recruited very young fighters, even teenagers. Further, the fighters in Syria and Iraq are far more diverse in terms of ancestral origin and race, with white Europeans comprising about 20 percent. No clear socio-economic profile exists either, with gang members from Europe's ethnic enclaves and drop-outs from universities and prestigious private schools joining up in equal measure. And, finally, there are more women because of militant groups' policy of getting young jihadists married very early. Some of these factors would seem to indicate a heightened risk—for example, the increased involvement of women would arguably expand the pool of possible attackers. Other factors are more ambiguous—young people on a jihadist "gap year" may return home regretting what they have done. Or they might want to go elsewhere and do something more when, if they survive, they leave or are expelled from Iraq and Syria.

Second, unlike before 9/11, when recruitment was a product of direct contact with exiled preachers based in the West, today, the recruitment of Westerners to fight in Syria and Iraq comes from extensive jihadist organizations in the West with deep roots and long histories of perpetrating violent attacks. The fighters in Syria and Iraq are thus deeply enmeshed in networks that were already responsible for violent incidents in West before the Syrian conflict captured their attention. That will increase the likelihood that returnees will be redirected to plots in the West or dispatched to other insurgencies abroad.

Finally, the jihadist ideology has changed from previous conflicts. In Afghanistan, the enemy was the Soviet Union. In Bosnia, it was the Serbs. In Somalia, it was the Ethiopians. In Syria and Iraq, the fight is primarily against other Muslims. And the jihadist insurgents in Syria and Iraq --irrespective of their factional differences—share a strategic interest in expanding the conflict to the whole of the Middle East so that they can undo the much-hated Sykes–Picot borders that effectively divided the collapsing Ottoman Empire into British and French protectorates. These terrorists recognize no borders or territorial limits to their fight. And that, too, increases the risk that the returnees may become a significant security risk at home.

OUNCE OF PREVENTION

So what can the West do? Above all, it cannot discount the threat of Western fighters in foreign conflicts. There are simply too many, and their ability and willingness to launch major attacks on the West is too great, to ignore.

Preventing people from leaving to fight with a terrorist organization in the first place is an urgent priority. All, or nearly all, of the newly minted Western-based jihadists from the Syrian and Iraqi conflicts hold Western passports. Current administrative controls target suspected terrorists and individuals who are known to have committed terrorist acts but who, for one reason or another, cannot be charged with criminal offenses. Measures range from impounding passports to imposing house arrests and curfews on individuals who are considered a risk to public safety.

To tackle the migration of a growing number of Western citizens to the frontlines of terrorist campaigns, though, preventive restrictions would have to be extended to hundreds if not thousands of people. Governments are already impounding passports in bulk, but ad hoc measures imposed in the absence of public debate will spawn a backlash against counterterrorism efforts down the road. Restricting the rights of citizens to travel is contrary to core Western values and, within the European Union, runs counter to years of efforts to promote mobility.

In the meantime, the West will have to calibrate its policing strategies to allow non-combatants and those with regrets to come home, while sorting out dangerous individuals for prosecution and detention. For pragmatic reasons—ranging from problems with obtaining evidence that meets the exacting standards of war crimes prosecutions to cost considerations—the authorities are likely to opt for prosecutions on lesser charges for which the evidence may be obtained closer to home. That is, they might focus on crimes committed in the West during the preparation for terrorist acts committed abroad. On the positive side, such a strategy could get dangerous terrorists off the street. On the negative, it will bring little comfort to the victims in Iraq and Syria, and Western states may look unwilling to punish their own citizens for crimes against non-Westerners.

A strategy for rehabilitation of post-conflict returnees who cannot be charged with criminal offenses is a must. As the conflict intensifies and casualties grow in Syria and Iraq, many of the less-experienced fighters, the teenagers and the women, will want to come home. Some will be traumatized. A few may even express regrets. Good counter-radicalization and rehabilitation strategies draw on the experience of dealing with gangs: Teams of law enforcement agents and social workers collaborate to provide mentors to former members. They also implement various types of direct supervision—bans on access to computers, for example, and limitations on the right to communicate with particular individuals. An advantage of the rehabilitation approach is that local authorities are able to keep a close watch on specific individuals and involve families.

Finally, there is the matter of providing justice to the victims. Westerners have participated in executions and crucifixions and raped and plundered in Syria and Iraq. Anticipating war crimes prosecutions of returnees, a number of countries (Sweden, France, Spain, and Canada) have recently enshrined crimes against humanity in their own countries' penal code, allowing domestic courts to prosecute severe crimes committed abroad. But such prosecutions require custody of the accused.

In other words, bringing the most hardened Western foreign fighters to justice would require their capture and rendition on a large scale. No precedent exists for legal renditions and judicial cooperation of this scale. In the past, European courts have spent years fighting over extraditions of terrorists wanted for trial elsewhere. Khaled al-Fawwaz, bin Laden's secretary, went about his business in London for more than a decade before he was extradited to stand trial in the United States on charges in connection with his role in the planning of the 1998 bombings of the U.S. embassies in Kenya and Tanzania. (The trial is set for November 3 in the Southern District of New York.)

The West is now faced with a foreign fighter problem of an unprecedented scale. It can expect that Westerners currently in Iraq and Syria will continue to commit atrocities abroad and will come home and attempt some kind of terrorist plot. It can expect most of the plots on Western soil to be thwarted and the perpetrators rounded up. That means, however, that the Western legal systems will have to finally adjust to dealing with unprecedented numbers of very dangerous people committing crimes for which the evidence is largely foreign, photographic, or found online. The risk of not doing so is already evident: a decade of terrorist recruitment in the West that drew thousands of young people into a violent revolutionary movement—all without provoking much of a response.

In the United States, the panic that Americans will soon be slaughtered in their beds by returning jihadists is barely concealed. That will not happen, but a realistic assessment of the scale of the threat nonetheless calls for extraordinary measures and international collaboration on the prevention, discovery, apprehension, and detention of the operatives that are responsible for funneling Western recruits into jihad campaigns abroad.

Research for this paper was supported by a grant from the U.S. Department of Justice, Office of Justice Program, The National Institute of Justice. (Award 2012 ZA-BX-0006.) Opinions or points of view expressed in this paper are those of the author and do not necessarily reflect the official position or policies of the U.S. Department of Justice.

Homeward Bound?

Don't Hype the Threat of Returning Jihadists

Daniel Byman and Jeremy Shapiro

O n May 24, 2014, a man opened fire inside the Jewish Museum in Brussels, quickly killing three people and fatally wounding a fourth before disappearing into the city's streets. The alleged perpetrator, a French citizen named Mehdi Nemmouche, who has since been arrested and charged with murder, had spent the previous year fighting with jihadist opposition groups in Syria. His attack appeared to mark the first time that the Syrian civil war had spilled over into the European Union. Many security officials in Europe and the United States fear that this strike foreshadowed a spate of terrorist attacks that the chaos in Syria—and now Iraq—could trigger.

The Syrian conflict has captured the imaginations and inflamed the passions of Muslims around the world, spurring thousands to join the mostly Sunni rebels resisting the Assad regime. The influx of volunteers has bolstered jihadist groups such as the Islamic State of Iraq and al-Sham (ISIS), also known as the Islamic State, a

DANIEL BYMAN is a Professor in the Security Studies Program at the Edmund A. Walsh School of Foreign Service at Georgetown University and a Senior Fellow at the Center for Middle East Policy at the Brookings Institution. Follow him on Twitter @dbyman.

JEREMY SHAPIRO is a Fellow with the Project on International Order and Strategy and at the Center on the United States and Europe at the Brookings Institution and a former member of the U.S. State Department's Policy Planning Staff. Follow him on Twitter @jyshapiro.

militant organization that swept across Syria's border into Iraq this past summer and proclaimed an Islamic caliphate.

Although most foreign fighters in Syria and Iraq come from the Arab world, a sizable contingent hails from the West's large Muslim communities; 19 million Muslims live in the EU, and more than two million call the United States home. Since the beginning of the Syrian civil war, about 2,500 people from those places (as well as Australia, Canada, and New Zealand) have traveled to Syria to fight, according to the Soufan Group, a U.S. security consulting firm.

Intelligence officials fear that these volunteers might return from the battlefield as terrorists trained to wage jihad against their home countries. Echoing these worries, Charles Farr, the director of the British Office for Security and Counter-Terrorism, described the Syrian war this past summer as "a very profound game changer" for the extremist threat to Europe. Similarly, James Comey, the director of the FBI, warned in May that the repercussions from the conflict might be "an order of magnitude worse" than those that followed the turbulence in Afghanistan during the 1980s and 1990s, which helped spur the formation of al Qaeda. And U.S. President Barack Obama was even more explicit during a prime-time speech to the nation on September 10, warning that "thousands of foreigners—including Europeans and some Americans" have joined ISIS militants and that "trained and battle-hardened, these fighters could try to return to their home countries and carry out deadly attacks."

But the threat presented by foreign fighters has been exaggerated, just as it was during several other conflicts in recent years. Over the last decade, the Iraq war in particular prompted similar warnings about a possible backlash that ultimately failed to materialize. In fact, the vast majority of Western Muslims who set out to fight in the Middle East today will not come back as terrorists. Many of them will never go home at all, instead dying in combat or joining new military campaigns elsewhere, or they will return disillusioned and not interested in bringing the violence with them.

Even among the rare individuals who do harbor such intentions, most will be less dangerous than they are feared to be because they will attract the attention of authorities before they can strike. It is telling that in the last two years alone, European security officials have disrupted at least five terrorist plots with possible links to Syrian foreign fighters, in locales ranging from Kosovo to the United Kingdom.

Still, the fact that the threat presented by returning Western jihadists will be less apocalyptic than commonly assumed should not lull authorities into complacency. Terrorism is a small-number phenomenon: even a few attackers can unleash horrific violence if they have the training and motivation. Moreover, the extremists' desire to strike the West could well be on the rise, fueled by the U.S. bombing of ISIS targets that began in August 2014. And because many more volunteers have traveled to Syria and Iraq than to any other conflict zone in the past, many more will ultimately come back.

Nevertheless, the danger posed by returning fighters is both familiar and manageable. Several measures could help further reduce it, including efforts to dissuade would-be volunteers from enlisting in the war to begin with and programs to reintegrate those who do into society when they return. Western intelligence agencies should also do more to disrupt common transit routes and track the militants who use them. And to maintain their vigilance, governments must adequately fund and equip their security services. Together, such measures will help prevent the violence in Syria and Iraq from spilling over into the West.

THERE AND BACK AGAIN

Western fighters who travel to faraway war zones generally follow a similar path as they make the transition from idealistic volunteers to seasoned militants. Most of those who begin the journey do not complete it; still, some do, and at each step Western officials can disrupt the progress of the few individuals who go all the way.

The first and most critical moment comes when a Muslim living in Europe or the United States, most often a young man, decides to join a distant military campaign. His motivations usually include a thirst for adventure and a desire to redress local and regional grievances in the Muslim world, rather than animosity toward the West. In Syria, most early volunteers aspired to defend the local population against the brutality of the Assad regime, not to wage global jihad.

This pattern began to change in 2013 as the war took on a sectarian cast; today, religious rivalry drives most of the recruits. The conflict has aggravated Sunni prejudices against Shiite Muslims—old sentiments that heated up during the U.S. war in Iraq and have now acquired new intensity. The ranks of militant Islamist groups in Syria swelled in late 2013 after prominent religious leaders, such as the Egyptian cleric Yusuf al-Qaradawi, called on all believers to defend Syrian Sunnis against the Assad regime and its Iranian and Shiite Lebanese allies.

In the summer of 2014, ISIS' stunning battlefield victories lent the organization credibility and enhanced its allure for the small but important Western community of young radicals it seeks to court. The group's calls for an Islamic emirate and its explicitly sectarian rhetoric have further radicalized the conflict. Such messages percolate through social media sites, including Facebook and Twitter, where jihadists often command large audiences. Isis, in particular, routinely churns out slick recruitment videos in English.

The second phase of the foreign fighter's path, traveling to the battlefield, has become remarkably easy to accomplish. Whereas reaching many earlier conflict destinations, such as Afghanistan, meant that Western volunteers had to face significant expenses and dangers, physically getting to Syria entails few sacrifices. Recruits can simply travel to Turkey—an easy trip by car, train, or plane requiring no visa for EU and U.S. citizens—and then cross into Syria along its vast and porous border. Social media also helps: ISIS and other radical groups, including one of ISIS' rivals, the Syrian al Qaeda affiliate Jabhat al-Nusra, offer ample online tips on how to contact them, including which Turkish hotels to pick in order to meet their travel facilitators.

The potency of the sectarian message and the cross-border flow of information and people help explain the unprecedented number of foreign fighters in Syria and Iraq today—greater than for any conflict in recent memory. Leading specialists on the topic, including Thomas Hegghammer of the Norwegian Defence Research Establishment and Peter Neumann, a British expert on radicalization, have estimated that the Syrian war has mobilized more European Islamists than all other foreign wars over the past 20 years combined. The U.S. share of the influx is smaller, but intelligence officials still believe that at least 100 Americans have joined the Syrian war since 2011.

The third step on the newcomer's path is to train and then actually fight on the battlefield. Training not only burnishes the recruit's practical skills; it also imbues him with a sense of solidarity with a larger cause. This experience deepens his indoctrination under the tutelage of sophisticated jihadists: Western security officials fear that a newcomer who might not start out as anti-Western could be manipulated by extremists to change his views, as happened with many fighters who went to Afghanistan in the 1980s and 1990s. The brutal combat that follows further hardens his resolve.

In the fourth step, the fighter returns home to keep the cycle going. Seasoned by battle, he acquires a new authority among his neighbors and followers on social media—a street cred that allows him to recruit and radicalize others and send them into the fray.

Finally, this veteran militant might decide to carry out a terrorist attack at home, turning his attention from foreign causes to real or imagined domestic injustices that may include, for example, insults against Islam, his home country's perceived oppression of Sunnis abroad, or the daily discrimination faced by Muslims. Analyzing the history of terrorist plots against the West, Hegghammer has found that when such strikes involved returned jihadists, they were both more likely to succeed and more lethal than attacks staged by homegrown terrorists who had not fought abroad.

MORE SMOKE THAN FIRE

Given how few obstacles preclude Western Muslims from joining faraway battles and returning home as terrorists, it might appear paradoxical that most conflicts in the Middle East have spawned barely any fighters who followed this path from start to finish. Syria and Iraq are likely to produce a similar pattern. True, the Syrian war bears many unique traits that significantly magnify the risk. Yet it is crucial not to exaggerate this threat, as governments and analysts have repeatedly done in the past, and to study historical and present-day intelligence in order to temper the dire predictions.

Iraq's previous war offers the most obvious example. Between 2003 and 2011, dozens of Muslims from Europe and the United States traveled to Iraq to fight Western forces. Some of them supported al Qaeda after it established a local affiliate in 2004 (a group known as al Qaeda in Iraq, which became the precursor to ISIS), and many grew more radicalized during their stay. In 2005, then CIA Director Porter Goss warned the Senate Select Committee on Intelligence that "Islamic extremists are exploiting the Iraqi conflict to recruit new anti-U.S. jihadists."

Yet despite such grim predictions, jihadist veterans of Iraq failed to perpetrate successful terrorist acts in the West. A few cases bore indirect evidence of a link to the conflict, including a bungled June 2007 strike on the Glasgow airport; investigators found that the attackers' cell phones contained the numbers of several operatives linked to al Qaeda in Iraq. But even in that case, U.S. officials ultimately judged the plot to be "al Qaeda–related, rather than al Qaeda–directed."

Syria and Iraq today are likely to echo this historical record. For one, many foreign volunteers will die in combat. The ferocity of the fighting in Syria and now Iraq—as the radicals battle the two countries' governments, the Syrian mainstream opposition, and, increasingly, one another—exceeds that of other recent conflicts. Researchers believe that the death toll among foreign volunteers in Syria has already surpassed that of the Iraq war, in which about five percent of all Western fighters are thought to have died. Of those who do survive, many will never return home, fearing arrest or choosing to wage jihad in other foreign lands. One European intelligence official estimated in an interview with us in May 2014 that from ten to 20 percent of foreign combatants have no plans to come back to their former countries of residence. (The official requested to remain anonymous because he was not authorized to discuss sensitive information.)

Furthermore, the Islamist groups active in Syria and Iraq, including ISIS, are not especially interested in attacking Europe or the United States. Instead, they are far more focused on fighting Shiites and local regimes. Many prominent Sunni clerics known for spurring holy warriors to action emphasize the importance of first winning such local contests before striking the West.

The case of Moner Mohammad Abusalha, the first American to carry out a suicide bombing in Syria, illustrates this phenomenon. Originally from Florida, Abusalha joined Jabhat al-Nusra after traveling to Syria in late 2013, and his death stirred U.S. officials' fears of a terrorist attack on domestic soil. An American citizen, Abusalha seemed to have been a perfect candidate to strike the United States. But Jabhat al-Nusra ordered him to attack Syrian government forces instead—a choice that clearly demonstrated the group's current priorities. The same logic applied to the British national suspected of killing the American journalists James Foley and Steven Sotloff this past August and September; even though the journalists' killer could have potentially wreaked havoc in London or elsewhere in Europe, ISIS assigned him a gruesome local task that would make him one of the most wanted men in the world, forever unable to return home.

The U.S. bombing of ISIS positions could change this sense of priorities. As the United States officially enters the fray against ISIS and U.S. involvement in the conflict deepens, the group may shift its priorities to attacking the U.S. homeland, or the West in general, out of revenge or defiance. But for now, ISIS' attention remains focused on its campaign against Syrian and Iraqi government forces.

Infighting among jihadist groups will further thin out the ranks of foreign recruits. Even as its fighters rolled into Iraq earlier this year, ISIS was embroiled in a bitter clash with Jabhat al-Nusra in Syria. Although both organizations follow Salafi jihadist ideology, ISIS rejected al Qaeda's leadership and aspects of its agenda, which led to a formal break between the two groups in February 2014. The resulting hostilities have already claimed more than 3,000 lives, according to the most conservative estimates, including the lives of four out of the five British volunteers killed in Syria during the first half of this year. Apart from augmenting the death toll, this kind of infighting breeds disillusionment among foreign recruits. European intelligence officials have found that some would-be volunteers often sour on the idea of enlisting when told that they might have to shoot at old neighbors from across the street, not Assad loyalists or the supposed apostates.

Another common reason for disillusionment is the horrors that Western fighters witness in the conflict zones, especially the Muslim-on-Muslim violence roiling Syria and Iraq. Recruits often set out in pursuit of "the T-shirt and the pictures" but come back terrified and even traumatized by what they have seen and experienced, according to the European intelligence official we interviewed.

With very few exceptions, Western Muslims who do return home rarely complete the transition to terrorist, even if they continue to vehemently oppose their countries' policies and values. In fact, the majority go on to lead largely ordinary lives. Hegghammer has found that only one in nine fighters who went abroad between 1990 and 2010 came back interested in attacking at home. The nature of the conflict in which they took part also plays a role. Combatants returning from Syria are likely to pose much less of a threat than veterans of al Qaeda's training facilities in Pakistan; because al Qaeda's goals are more explicitly anti-Western than those of ISIS, al Qaeda fighters will account for a larger share of the plots in Europe and the United States.

The few individuals who remain bent on violence after returning from Syria and Iraq will often be easy targets for counterterrorism officials. For one, their heavy reliance on social media will become a double-edged sword. By openly publicizing and bragging about their activities online, these people identify themselves to security services and at times supply valuable intelligence data: their group affiliation, intentions, and associates. Officials can also glean useful information by studying their lists of friends and followers. As the European official explained to us, some potential terrorists remain "totally invisible" to authorities until they set out for Syria or Iraq and expose themselves online.

What's more, former foreign fighters contemplating violence at home could find that their experience in Syria and Iraq has left them ill equipped for the task. Although many learn some guerilla-warfare skills, such as handling small arms, they often lack the knowledge most useful for mounting successful terrorist attacks: how to conduct surveillance, avoid detection, and build a clandestine network. And when they operate in groups—a necessity for executing large-scale strikes—they are even more likely to come to the security services' attention.

Even the sole successful attack in Brussels demonstrated why fighters returning from the Syrian war pose less of a danger than is often supposed. In executing his assault, Nemmouche acted alone, which allowed him to escape authorities' notice but also limited the damage he was able to cause. And although he had picked up some combat skills in Syria, Nemmouche appeared to lack any knowledge of concealment or evasion. He never got rid of his Kalashnikov rifle following the shooting; instead, he wrapped it in an ISIS flag and boarded a bus on a well-known and well-policed cannabis-smuggling route from Amsterdam to Marseille, leading to his quick arrest.

Finally, foreign fighters may be reluctant to bring violence back home for the simple reason that doing so could endanger their friends and relatives. In an interview with *The New York Times*, a friend of Abdisalan Hussein Ali, a Somali American from Minnesota who blew himself up in a 2011 attack on African Union troops in

Mogadishu, recalled a revealing statement Ali had made two years before he left for Somalia. He would never attack the United States, Ali had said, since "my mom could be walking down the street."

BREAKING THE CYCLE

Analyzing each step of the journey taken by Westerners who travel to fight in Syria and Iraq—as well as the factors that prevent them from staging attacks back home—suggests several policy measures that could further reduce the risk. First, Western security services should step up their efforts to dissuade the recruits from volunteering in the first place. One model for how to do this is a government-run program in Denmark that allows officials to seek out and speak with potential recruits in an informal setting, often in conjunction with family members and local community leaders. The goal of such conversations is always to persuade, not coerce. Because the cooperation of families and communities is so vital to this task, officials are careful to press home the message that the Muslim population is a valued part of the solution, rather than the problem. And if individuals do volunteer and go abroad to fight with militants, governments could take measures to prevent their return; one program proposed by British Prime Minister David Cameron in September intends to accomplish just that by confiscating the passports of suspected radical fighters.

Western governments should also do more to make it harder for would-be jihadists to reach Syria and Iraq through Turkey. Until recently, Ankara's opposition to the Assad regime made Turkey a tacit supporter of fighters streaming across its border. But the rise of ISIS and the looming threat of extremism on Turkey's own soil have made its government more receptive to Western calls to halt the flow. The United States and European countries should use this opportunity to devise a better system for sharing information with Turkish intelligence and police agencies. For a start, Western officials could issue travel alerts for specific individuals and encourage Turkey to bar them from entering the country or crossing into Syria from its territory.

Western security agencies should also do everything they can to sow doubt in the minds of extremist leaders in Syria and Iraq about the true loyalties of Western Muslim volunteers. This could be accomplished by publicizing intelligence, either obtained from former recruits or even falsely generated by officials themselves, about the degree to which Western security services have infiltrated the jihadists' ranks. If extremist militias come to view foreigners as potential spies or disseminators of corrupting influences, they might assign Western volunteers to noncombat roles, test their allegiances by offering them the one-way ticket of suicide bombings, or even avoid enlisting them altogether.

Western agencies also need to strengthen their currently inconsistent methods of monitoring returnees and identifying individuals who pose the greatest threat, as well as coordinating these efforts among themselves. The most dangerous returnees need to be closely monitored and, if possible, jailed. (Specific charges would vary by country and could include, for example, membership in a prohibited terrorist group.) But pursuing criminal prosecutions of all Western Muslims who fight abroad could backfire. Although it would temporarily neutralize former combatants, it might also alienate them even further—and, in Europe, expose them to the influence of hardened jihadists, who are amply represented in Europe's prison populations. Even the mere threat of jail might make a former fighter feel that he has less to lose and push him toward violence. Indiscriminate prosecution would also turn Muslim communities against the government, making them less likely to identify violent radicals in their midst.

Western governments should instead focus on reintegrating former fighters, despite the political difficulty of spending public resources on people whom many consider terrorists. Some returnees will require psychological counseling and treatment for posttraumatic stress disorder; failing to provide it might make them more dangerous than they otherwise would be. If fear of prosecution prevents former fighters from seeking counseling and treatment, they will be less able to reintegrate into civilian life and leave their violent pasts behind.

Last, even though the threat from returning jihadists has been overblown, Western governments still need to devote considerable resources to the problem. Keeping track of the vast roster of suspects that the intelligence agencies must maintain under surveillance at any given time will be exceptionally taxing on both budgets and personnel. But because the influx of foreign fighters to Syria and Iraq exceeds those of previous conflicts, the number of intelligence and police officials dedicated to the problem should grow in parallel. For government agencies, the challenge often lies not in accessing or gathering information about the returnees but in swiftly processing and analyzing it before reacting.

Western governments should also continue to seek ways to alleviate civilian suffering in Syria and Iraq. Many foreign fighters remain driven by a genuine desire to defend Syrians against the brutality of the Assad regime, even as sectarianism takes increasing sway over rival groups. Encouraging charitable activities, identifying legitimate channels for delivering humanitarian aid, and otherwise helping prevent unnecessary loss of civilian life could go a long way toward stemming the flow of foreigners to the war zone.

As long as the Syrian civil war and the ISIS offensive in Iraq continue, however, some fallout in the West appears inevitable. Terrorism is an unfortunate feature of modern life that cannot be eradicated; it can only be mitigated. Indeed, the Obama administration's decision to intervene against ISIS makes the group more likely to try to expand its list of immediate targets. Yet it is important to avoid panic and to recognize that both the United States and the EU have fended off the worst outcomes in the past and will likely continue to do so.

Measures to reduce the threat of terrorism can and should be improved. But the standard of success cannot be eliminating risk in its totality. If it is, Western governments are doomed to failure and, worse, to an overreaction that will breed far more dangerous policy mistakes.

ISIS' Gruesome Gamble

Why the Group Wants a Confrontation with the United States

Barak Mendelsohn

The Islamic State of Iraq and al-Sham (ISIS), which is also called the Islamic State, is on the march. Two months after first sweeping through northern and central Iraq, it has started to push onward to Erbil, the seat of the Kurdish Regional Government. Along the way, it triggered a severe humanitarian crisis among Iraq's Yezidi and Christian minorities and caused massive panic across the Kurdish autonomous region, which forced a reluctant United States to intervene. ISIS has also used its momentum to continue its expansion in Syria and, for a few days, even managed to hold parts of the Lebanese border city of Arsal. More confident than ever, ISIS is taking on a broad array of enemies, including the Iraqi, Syrian, and Lebanese militaries; Iraqi and Lebanese Shia militias; Kurds from Iraq, Syria, and Turkey; and Islamist and secular Syrian opposition forces. Now even U.S. air power is joining the fray.

From a military perspective, ISIS' willingness to fight so many groups on so many fronts is impressive. In part, its boldness was made possible by the weakness of many of its rivals. The huge store of deadly, high-quality weapons that the group picked up on its

BARAK MENDELSOHN is an Associate Professor of political science at Haverford College and a Research Fellow at Harvard Kennedy School's Belfer Center for Science and International Affairs. Follow him on Twitter @BarakMendelsohn.

march through Iraq has helped as well. Finally, ISIS has also demonstrated a surprising ability to rearrange and redeploy forces as the group's operational needs change. Its reputation for military prowess (and brutality) has only grown, which in turn has further weakened resistance to its moves and sent civilians running whenever ISIS forces got close.

ISIS' relatively unimpeded march toward Erbil caught the White House and many other observers by surprise. Most had expected that the jihadist group would concentrate its efforts in Iraq on Baghdad, the capital and a historical seat of the Abbasid Caliphate, where numerous Sunni reside. They also believed that the Kurdish peshmarga forces were strong enough to deter ISIS attacks and would be able to block its advance if deterrence failed. That turns out to have been wrong, a miscalculation that forced the Obama administration's hand. Still, because ISIS' move provoked a U.S. bombardment, some believe it might well be its undoing.

For that reason, ISIS' strategy might seem like a surprising overreach. It is entirely consistent, however, with the path the group charted early on, which tended toward the bold and risky. In fact, ISIS' recent moves are simply a continuation of prior efforts to expand its control over new territory and natural resources (primarily oil fields and water dams that it can use for income and tools of war), enforce its harsh ideology, and strengthen its own primacy within the jihadi camp.

For now, it is impossible to say whether ISIS intended to provoke the United States to intervene or simply miscalculated. But it is hard to believe ISIS did not understand that threatening the capital of Iraqi Kurdistan would mean directly challenging the U.S. alliance with the Kurds and potentially provoking it to fight. Indeed, it is likely that ISIS viewed such a challenge as a win-win situation.

If the United States had failed to protect its allies, ISIS forces would have been able to advance deep into Kurdish territory and masses of "undesirable" non-Sunni inhabitants would have fled. The demonstration of U.S. timidity would also have given ISIS a boost as it set its sights on Jordan, another anxious U.S. ally in need of Washington's defense.

If the United States decided to step in on behalf of its allies—as it did—then ISIS must have believed that it would be able to strengthen its position within the jihadi camp. ISIS could use the bombings as evidence that the United States is waging a war on Islam, and to portray itself as the defender of Muslims from "Crusader" aggression. In other words, ISIS would steal a page right out of al Qaeda's playbook. And that puts more pressure on al Qaeda. After all, if ISIS wins vast territory in the heart of the Middle East, implements Islamic governance, and battles apostate regimes and their backers, al Qaeda will—after refusing to do so—have to give its full support to ISIS. Already, ISIS supporters are calling all jihadi forces to stand behind Omar al-Baghdadi, the leader of ISIS. As a result, the flow of fighters abandoning al Qaeda affiliates to join ISIS, which U.S. intelligence has already observed, is likely to increase. Moreover, leaders of al Qaeda franchises will come under greater pressure to shift allegiance from al Qaeda to ISIS.

Of course, getting the United States involved carries considerable risks. ISIS does not have an answer to American airpower. From the air, the United States is capable of delivering painful blows that can significantly degrade the group. And by supporting Kurdish forces on the ground, U.S. intervention could even reverse ISIS' advances in the north. But U.S. President Barack Obama's caution when it comes to foreign interventions, and his obvious distaste for getting entangled in Iraq again, appear to have mitigated the risks for ISIS. Indeed, the United States seems intent on the most minimal intervention possible, striking very few targets, and aiming to create deterrence more than rolling back ISIS advances on the ground. Moreover, Obama's aversion to doing anything in Syria means that ISIS-controlled territories there will be a safe haven for the group no matter what happens in Iraq.

Although the push against the Kurds can be seen as serving the Islamic State's strategic objectives, the persecution of minorities, particularly the beginning of a genocidal drive against the Yezidis, should be viewed not only as an effort to intimidate the opponents of ISIS, but also as the fulfillment of ISIS' radical ideology, which includes special taxes for minorities, forced deportations or, as in the case of the Yezidis, a choice between conversion or death. This ideology is an integral part of ISIS' broader effort to implement Islamic governance and has some precedents in its actions in Syria. In the absence of concerted international action, it will continue to oppress, chase away, and, in the worst cases, kill minorities under its rule.

ISIS has been clear about its expansionist and exclusionary Caliphate project, and now that truth has finally sunk in with the Obama administration. Getting involved in Iraq carries risks, but if the United States will not lead—and from the front this time— the ISIS threat will only grow. A lasting solution to the problem requires deep political changes in Iraq and, just as important, in Syria, which Washington has largely ignored. Such changes are unlikely to materialize fast enough to answer an urgent threat. In the meantime, although a comprehensive aerial campaign could weaken ISIS considerably, the narrow scope of U.S. strikes will provide only modest and insufficient relief. Fighting ISIS will inevitably generate some resentment against the United States. However, the danger that would result from allowing ISIS to expand unchecked is far worse. Unless the United States is willing to walk away from the Middle East for good, it will have to face ISIS head on. And doing so will cost much more the longer the United States waits.

ISIS' Worst Nightmare

Why the Group Is Not Trying to Provoke a U.S. Attack

By Robin Simcox

To fulfill his vow to "destroy" the Islamic State of Iraq and al-Sham (ISIS), U.S. President Barack Obama will have to make a lengthy military commitment to Iraq and Syria. So far, however, the United States has limited its involvement to air strikes in Iraq and some military assistance to Iraqi and Kurdish forces on the ground. Obama's speech this month also raised the prospect of air strikes in Syria.

Yet, within the halls of Western power, there are still those who regard using military force against ISIS as a mistake, believing that it will bolster the jihadists' narrative of the West vs. Islam and aid ISIS propaganda—especially if there are civilian casualties. In turn, ISIS will find it easier to recruit new members. For that reason, some have argued, ISIS was hoping to provoke a showdown with the United States all along.

Nothing could be further from the truth. Looking at the group's recent history, it is clear that the last thing ISIS would want is for the United States to step up its military efforts in Iraq. After all, it was the U.S. military—in conjunction with Sunni tribes—that crushed the group's emerging network in Iraq in late 2006 and early 2007. By 2008, the group's estimated 15,000 membership had been eviscerated by the death of 2,400 of its members and the

ROBIN SIMCOX is a Research Fellow at the Henry Jackson Society.

capture of another 8,800. At the time of the U.S. troop withdrawal from Iraq in December 2011, the network now known as ISIS had between 800 and 1,000 members

Although the ongoing civil war in Syria may have reenergized ISIS, it was the U.S. withdrawal that really turned the group's fortunes around. For example, with the U.S. departure, Iraqi special forces lost access to American intelligence and helicopter transportation, significantly diminishing their abilities to carry out nighttime counterterrorism operations. On the political side, Iraqi Prime Minister Nouri al-Maliki took the withdrawal as his cue to purge senior military figures whom the United States had trusted and replace them with vastly less competent loyalists. By October 2012, the Iraqi jihadist network had taken advantage of this to more than double in size and virtually double the amount of attacks it was carrying out a week.

That is why ISIS' activities in Iraq—particularly the beheadings of the American journalists James Foley and Steven Sotloff, which members of government, including Representative Adam Schiff (D-Cal.), a member of the House Intelligence Committee, have argued were meant to tempt Obama into action—are really meant to deter the United States.

In the video of Foley's beheading, for example, a British ISIS fighter suspected of carrying out the murder claims to be retaliating against U.S. bombing raids and the United States' attempt "to deny the Muslims their rights of living in safety under the Islamic caliphate." In the second video, Sotloff is made to ask whether U.S. citizens are interested in another war against ISIS having already "spent billions of U.S. taxpayers' dollars and . . . lost thousands of our troops." The British ISIS fighter warns governments looking to assist the United States to "back off and leave our people alone." The video then cuts to an image of the British hostage, David Haines. These videos, understandably, did not lead to a change in Western policy, and Haines was killed next. The rhetoric in the video of his killing is similar to that in the Foley and Sotloff videos. The British ISIS fighter explicitly references how the Western military campaign in Iraq will lead to "another bloody and unwinnable war," and that by continuing the fight against ISIS, the West will cause more British citizens to die. Alan Henning, another British man captured by ISIS, is identified as the next potential victim.

ISIS' ideological forebears have used similar tactics with Western hostages. When American citizen Nicholas Berg and British citizen Kenneth Bigley were beheaded by Abu Musab al-Zarqawi's network in 2004, Zarqawi was not trying to draw the United States and United Kingdom more deeply into the Iraq war. (There were already over 140,000 U.S. troops in Iraq at the time of Berg's murder.) Rather, he was trying to weaken public support for the war and test whether the West had the stomach for this kind of fight. For example, prior to his death, Bigley was forced to read a statement saying that "Iraqis don't like foreign troops on their soil walking down the street with guns—it's not right and it's not fair. We need to pull the troops out."

ISIS also has a sound strategic reason for trying to deter further Western military escalation. Retaining and expanding its territory is the group's main goal. The longer the caliphate endures, the more credible it seems and the more recruits it can attract. The end result of ramped up Western military action is likely to be the loss of much of ISIS' territory and the collapse of its caliphate, shattering its image of strength and the inevitability of its advance. This was the case with al Qaeda franchises in Somalia, Yemen, and Mali in recent years. These groups, although not able to match ISIS in terms of numbers and ability to hold land, have all relinquished territory after military reverses. In other words, a new war would likely send ISIS back to where it was before 2014: it would be a security threat, especially to Iraq, but no longer a credible challenger to al Qaeda in terms of its reach and capacity.

In turn, if the West is serious about defeating ISIS, the group cannot be allowed to hold on to the territory it now controls. Local forces are not up to the task of reclaiming land from ISIS, and regional actors are showing little interest in intervention. Since ISIS is not going to give up without a fight, significant Western military involvement is required. Some argue that such involvement will increase the prospect of ISIS retribution in the West. Yet ISIS was a threat to the West long before American air strikes. Over the last decade, the group has been connected to multiple terrorist attacks in Europe, offered financial reward for the murder of European citizens, and was linked to a plan to transport chemical weapons into the West. Allowing its members control of a safe haven from which it could recruit and train new fighters only increases the threat that ISIS poses.

It is true that there will be unpleasant consequences for reengaging in Iraq. It would be naive to think there will no price to pay for taking on a terrorist army that is killing its enemies with impunity, controlling a significant territory in two strategically important countries, and whose fighters have a stated desire to kill Westerners. There is also an emerging consensus that any successful strategy to comprehensively weaken ISIS will take years—a commitment for which public support is unclear.

None of this, however, means that avoiding conflict there will bolster Western security. By not acting, the West would be relying on the group to self-destruct. And that is too risky. For his part, Obama has shown a willingness to take military action, even though it means reversing his previous policies in Iraq and Syria. Yet there may be another reversal ahead. Obama has vowed to "destroy" ISIS without using ground troops in a combat role. These two things may yet prove mutually exclusive.

Staying Out of Syria

Why the United States Shouldn't Enter the Civil War—But Why It Might Anyway

Steven Simon

U.S. President Barack Obama has taken pains to avoid being drawn into Syria's civil war. He does not appear convinced that the United States has sufficient strategic interests in Syria to warrant—let alone sustain—another long-term commitment of military force to shape the outcome of what is a complicated and many-sided struggle. Even as Obama has expanded the U.S. war against the Islamic State of Iraq and al-Sham (ISIS) to include targets in Syria, then, he has tried to circumscribe the mission. The aim is to battle ISIS without either aiding or fighting the regime of Syrian President Bashar al-Assad. But the balancing act is proving difficult. The United States could soon face a choice between appearing to provide tacit support to Syrian government forces and joining the fight against them.

The United States has long faced pressure to intervene in Syria's civil war; it dates back to 2011, even before early skirmishes turned into high-intensity combat. Then as now, the administration's stance was cautious. At that stage, it looked as though Assad might go the way of Tunisia's Zine el-Abidine Ben Ali or Egypt's Hosni Mubarak. Given the brittleness of the Assad regime, the use

STEVEN SIMON is Senior Fellow at the Middle East Institute in Washington, D.C.

of force seemed unnecessary. And in any case, there was no appetite for a bidding war with Iran for Syria.

Yet the Assad regime proved more resilient than many expected. Interest in arming and training the Syrian rebels only grew, despite Washington's evident inability to wield influence over the hundreds of partially radicalized armed groups already proliferating in Syria, let alone mold them into a unified opposition army. As we now know from multiple memoirs, Obama overruled his secretaries of defense and state, who urged him to do more to arm those rebels in late 2012.

Calls to help overthrow Assad grew louder after his regime used chemical weapons against civilian populations in August 2013. Again, Obama declined to strike once the United Kingdom opted out of military involvement and Russia proffered a diplomatic alternative that eventually stripped the regime of its chemical weapons. The resulting mix of disappointment and anger at home over a forgone opportunity to strike Assad's forces was bound to make it harder for Obama to say no the next time a challenge arose.

And it did. Following reports that ISIS, which had just overrun the western provinces of Iraq and entered Mosul, was intent on the genocide of a religious minority in Iraq, the United States immediately launched air strikes to protect the vulnerable and safeguard American officials in Erbil. The use of force never comes without unintended consequences, and in this case, the attacks precipitated the murder of two Americans, which in turn amplified calls for military escalation.

Even so, in that early phase of U.S. military operations, the air campaign was in the service of a clear, if limited, interest in protecting the American strategic investment in Iraq by relieving jihadist pressure on Baghdad and pushing the divisive prime minister, Nouri al-Maliki, out of office. To the extent that prospective strikes in Syria were discussed, their narrow aim was to deprive what was seen as an Iraqi insurgency of its sanctuary across the border. As the objective expanded to include the destruction of ISIS, though, U.S. strikes have extended as far west as the outskirts of Syria's former cultural and economic capital of Aleppo, now a vast rubble field contested by the regime and a congeries of rebel militias, and as far north as the Turkish border.

These attacks, with their implied promise of close air support for non-jihadist fighters assailed by ISIS, have brought the United States perilously close to entry into the Syrian civil war. Turkish Prime Minister Ahmet Davutoglu's recent offer to send Turkish troops into Syria if the United States would, in return, directly attack the Assad regime—and Ankara's wrangling with the United States over access to Turkish air bases—has only added to sustained pressure coming from the Gulf allies.

The key question is: What happens if one of the non-jihadist opposition groups that the United States is aiding in the fight against ISIS requests urgent assistance against the Assad regime? If the United States fails to come to the group's aid, the support the United States enjoys among these groups by virtue of its airpower and train-and-equip efforts would swiftly fade. But if the United States accedes to the request, then it unequivocally becomes a combatant in the civil war. And if the United States consents to Turkey's proposal for a safe haven within Syria for refugees and possibly as a base for an opposition army—essentially a tethered goat stratagem designed to trigger regime attacks that American planes would then have to repel—Washington would become even more deeply engaged in the conflict.

The civil war in Syria does, of course, endanger some U.S. strategic interests. Iraq, for example, is one, and the United States has acted decisively to protect it. Jordan is another, given the Hashemite Kingdom's historically close relationship with the United States (it is a Major non-NATO Ally) and its close security links to Israel. The influx of Syrian refugees into that country is a threat to its stability, as is the receptive audience ISIS has found among the unemployed youth in its impoverished desert cities. In response, the United States ramped up its already considerable economic and military aid to Jordan and, last December, deployed 6,000 soldiers to Jordan for a large-scale exercise. Likewise, Lebanon has received billions in military aid from Riyadh, while Hezbollah fields a force that has faced the Israeli army on the battlefield and is ideologically primed to contest ISIS attempts to establish a beachhead in Lebanon. And between 2012 and now, the United States has provided nearly $3 billion in humanitarian aid for displaced Syrians.

But there is no equivalent U.S. interest in Syria per se. For 40 years, it was a strategic ally of the Soviets; it then switched its allegiance to another strategic adversary, Iran. Most Syrians are skeptical of U.S. intentions, owing to decades of support for Israel as well as the United States' hands-off approach to the civil war. Assad's outreach to Washington, which came only a short time before rebellion broke out, was too little, too late. There is no history of cooperation, shared causes, or solemn commitments. Syria is of no military value to the United States, which has ample basing and access options throughout the Mediterranean rim, and of negligible economic value.

It would be strategically useful to completely deny Syrian territory to Iran, but the attempt to do so would likely increase Iran's military involvement and heighten sectarian tensions, while complicating efforts to reach a deal on Iran's nuclear program. Although some terrorist attacks in the West, such as the one just carried out in Canada, will certainly arise from a jihadized Syria, the long-term investment the United States has made in homeland security and intelligence programs, combined with air strikes that keep ISIS conspirators in Syria and Iraq off balance, should contain the problem without the burden of a new expeditionary commitment.

Hence the administration's dilemma. On the one hand, military intervention in the civil war would commit the United States to an expensive and ongoing enterprise unrelated to a strategic interest in Syria itself. On the other, it might prove necessary in order to bring other countries' firepower to bear against ISIS. While Washington debates the question, however, its air operations deep in Syrian territory could propel the United States into the civil war without a considered or explicit decision.

A tragic choice is emerging between restraint against ISIS to avoid entanglement in Syria's civil war or full engagement against ISIS with an eye to regime change and the reconstruction and stabilization of a devastated country. After Afghanistan, Iraq, and Libya, we have a rough idea of what such an effort would entail and of the elusiveness of lasting gains. A decision to go all the way is one that should be taken only with the greatest of caution and a careful assessment of the gap between our resources and our maximalist goals and the gap between these goals and our strategic interests. At this stage, all these considerations remain badly out of sync and quite possibly irreconcilable.

The Hollow Coalition

Washington's Timid European Allies

Raphael Cohen and Gabriel Scheinmann

Three months since U.S. bombs first struck Islamic State of Iraq and al-Sham (ISIS) targets in Iraq, the Obama administration has touted its 62-country coalition as a crowning achievement. Although this number might seem impressive, however, it is misleading. Of the 62 nominal allies for Operation Inherent Resolve (as the campaign is now called), only 16 have actually committed military forces, and only 11 have conducted offensive operations to date. Many appear willing to pay lip service to U.S. President Barack Obama's condemnation of ISIS, only to ignore his subsequent call to arms.

Most disconcerting is the meekness of Washington's supposedly stalwart European allies. The European countries that have deployed forces to fight ISIS are contributing less today than they did three years ago in Operation Unified Protector in Libya—and even in that conflict, the United States was indispensable to the mission. France is a case in point. It fired the opening shot in the Libyan campaign and sent to the front 29 planes and six warships, including an aircraft carrier. Today, however, it has devoted only 11 planes and one warship to fighting ISIS. Similarly, the United Kingdom sent 28 planes to Libya in 2011 but only eight to Iraq this year. And whereas a total of 13 European countries had contributed either ships or planes to the struggle against the

---

RAPHAEL COHEN and GABRIEL SCHEINMANN are defense analysts in Washington, D.C.

Muammar al-Qaddafi regime, only five have done the same in the war on ISIS.

Nowhere is European reticence more apparent than in the share of airstrikes. In Libya, **90 percent** of the air raids were carried out by Washington's coalition partners, destroying more than 6,000 targets. This percentage puts the U.S. allies' current share—approximately 10 percent of over **800 strikes** conducted so far in Iraq and Syria—to shame. The share of the EU is even smaller, since some strikes were conducted by other coalition partners: Australia, Canada, and five Arab states. And this time around, the European countries are openly admitting that their contribution would be mere window-dressing. As British Foreign Secretary Philip Hammond acknowledged in a particularly candid testimony in early September, the British contribution aimed primarily at bolstering "a political coalition of nations" rather than changing the military tide. Seventy years after British and American soldiers landed in nearly equal numbers on the beaches of Normandy, even the United Kingdom, which has Europe's most powerful military, recognizes that it can no longer be decisive on the battlefield.

SLIMMING THE RANKS

Such an underwhelming European response is puzzling. After all, European security interests should dictate an even more robust effort against ISIS than against the Qaddafi regime. For one, ISIS represents a much more immediate security threat. An estimated **3,000 European jihadists** have joined ISIS' ranks, and many of them have returned home bent on further violence, including one that killed four people in an attack on the Jewish Museum of Belgium in Brussels this past May. Second, ISIS militants, unlike Qaddafi, have explicitly threatened to attack European countries and have killed European citizens. The Qaddafi regime, on the other hand, had signed a number of lucrative oil deals with European companies before it fell; it also largely abandoned its unconventional weapons program and ended its sponsorship of terrorism in Europe. And third, unlike the United States, Europe was mostly spared the Iraq war's direct toll (accounting for just 282 of the 4,804 coalition casualties, most borne by the United Kingdom) and therefore does not suffer from battle fatigue.

The reason for the European countries' lackluster effort lies not in their war weariness or a miscalculation of their interests but in their vastly diminished military capacity—the result of deep cuts to their defense budgets. Put simply, Washington's European allies no longer have the strength to conduct and sustain even medium-sized military operations.

Europe's military spending plummeted after the Cold War, and the recent recession has prompted five consecutive years of further cuts in absolute terms. The defense budgets of most NATO nations now stand at their lowest point since 2001, according to the Stockholm International Peace Research Institute. Currently, only Estonia, Greece, and the United Kingdom meet NATO's mutually agreed-upon target for defense spending—defined as two percent of GDP—even though member states reaffirmed their commitment to that target at a NATO summit in September. In 2013, European NATO members (a group that includes Turkey) spent a combined $270 billion on defense, which is less than half of the annual U.S. defense budget. As a result, the United States will likely dedicate more money to Operation Inherent Resolve than the majority of European NATO states will allocate to security and defense in the whole year.

NOT ON TARGET

The Libyan campaign, which some observers have praised as an example of European military effectiveness and used to urge more European involvement in Syria, represents just the opposite. In fact, it underscores Europe's declining military clout by demonstrating that EU countries can mount a successful military operation only under a best-case scenario. Cases that, like Iraq and Syria today, present greater strategic and logistic challenges quickly bring Europe's vulnerabilities to the fore.

Several factors combined to make Libya the perfect staging ground for a European military intervention. First, the operation took place just off the European coast, well within the range of European air bases. By contrast, to strike ISIS targets, European planes must fly out of Cyprus, Jordan, and the Persian Gulf countries—a far more difficult task from the logistical and diplomatic standpoints. Second, Libya's vast stretches of open desert between population centers made for an easier operating environment. Although western Iraq is likewise sparsely populated, ISIS strongholds such as the cities of Mosul (in northern Iraq) and Raqqa (in Syria) are not. Finally, unlike Qaddafi's army, which had lost its edge long before the West intervened, ISIS fighters are well funded, well armed, and able to score impressive victories.

Yet even in that favorable situation, European countries found their logistic and intelligence capabilities stretched to the limit, forcing them to rely on U.S. forces. Noting these shortfalls, the 2013 edition of *The Military Balance,* an annual assessment of global defense capabilities published by the International Institute for Strategic Studies, concluded that the Libyan operation highlighted Europe's military decline rather than heralding Europe's emergence as a capable security actor.

Furthermore, after the initial victory in Libya, it quickly became clear that the Western operation there was not a success. Libya is in a state of anarchy. Its capital has fallen to Islamist militant factions, its parliament has fled, and its oil production hovers far below prewar levels. Meanwhile, nearby European countries are struggling to stem the tide of refugees streaming across Libyan borders. As just one example, Italy plans to discontinue its year-long search-and-rescue operation in the central Mediterranean, which has saved the lives of more than 150,000 migrants. Its place will be taken by the new Operation Triton, funded by eight member states and intended to "ensure effective border control." In other words, only three years after they intervened to save Libyans from oppression, the European nations find themselves focused on keeping those same individuals out.

A whole array of other factors strengthens Europe's reluctance to enter such conflicts in the future. The EU is saddled by debt (with an average debt-to-GDP ratio of 88 percent) and faces declining birth rates and graying populations, forcing governments to devote funds to caring for their retirees rather than modernizing armies. Further, growing political discord at home—including a rise of far-right eurosceptic political parties—makes European leaders even more reluctant to join costly international military endeavors. Even new threats, such as ISIS or an armed separatist rebellion in eastern Ukraine, are likely to pale in comparison with Europe's other problems.

A SPENT FORCE

The disappointing European contribution to Operation Inherent Resolve offers several lessons. The tepid response highlights just how far European military capabilities have deteriorated. Even though some states have made modest increases to their defense budgets in response to Russia's actions in Ukraine, these changes fall far short of reversing Europe's military decline. The continued stagnation of European economies, dismal demographic trends, and lack of political will make the resurrection of Europe as a military power nearly impossible for the foreseeable future.

For that reason, the United States ought to reevaluate its future expectations of European military contributions, especially to out-of-area missions, and begin planning accordingly. With time, European states will become even less forthcoming with their military support. Washington's European allies simply lack the capability to contribute in a meaningful way, even in response to worthy military missions or security challenges on their doorstep. Washington should thus focus on enlisting allies that are not only willing to join a coalition but capable of contributing resources and personnel to it.

Finally, the war on ISIS underscores Washington's unique global position of leadership when it comes to defending the West. Its allies count on it to project power globally and even to come to their aid when they cannot defend themselves. For all its budget woes, political gridlock, and desire to pivot away from the world's problems, the United States will continue to find itself doing the heavy lifting—whether combating ISIS or deterring a recidivist Russia—for the foreseeable future. Simply put, there is no one else.

Hammer and Anvil

How to Defeat ISIS

Robert A. Pape, Keven Ruby, and Vincent Bauer

At the top of U.S. Secretary of Defense Ashton Carter's agenda for 2015 is stopping the Islamic State of Iraq and al-Sham (ISIS). Many critics assert that the current policy of limited air strikes is insufficient to defeat or seriously weaken ISIS and have offered radical alternatives. However, these "cures" are far worse than the disease. The best plan is to aggressively move forward within the broad parameters of the current strategy, building on its successes and vastly diminishing ISIS' power and influence by the time U.S. President Barack Obama leaves office in two years.

GREAT EXPECTATIONS

There are two prominent (and nearly polar opposite) alternatives to current policy. At one extreme, CFR Senior Fellow Max Boot calls for the deployment of up to 30,000 U.S. ground combat troops, a U.S.-enforced no-fly zone, and incentives to enlist Turkey as an active military partner in the fight—all in order to push the

ROBERT A. PAPE is the author of Bombing to Win: Air Power and Coercion in War and a Professor at the University of Chicago, where he heads the Chicago Project on Security and Terrorism.

KEVEN RUBY is Research Director of CPOST. VINCENT BAUER is Research Analyst at CPOST.

Kurds, the Shia-dominated Iraqi security forces, and Sunnis to work together to roll back ISIS from its strongholds in Iraq and Syria. At the other extreme, retired Air Force Lieutenant General David Deptula argues that a vastly expanded air campaign against ISIS' leadership and economic and military centers of gravity can so weaken the group that a broad Sunni resistance will quickly rise up, making any U.S. Special Forces on the ground unnecessary.

These proposals are as unrealistic as they are ambitious. No doubt, Washington would love to find a silver bullet to quickly defeat ISIS in Syria and Iraq, but neither of the proposals is likely to work as advertised. There are over 20 million Sunnis in Syria and Iraq, a large fraction of which are now cooperating (passively or actively) with ISIS and would fight hard to avoid Kurdish and Shia domination, much less American control. Meanwhile, sending in U.S. ground forces might help win bits of territory along the current perimeter of ISIS-held territory, but it is unlikely to weaken the group in the heart of the Sunni-majority areas. Even worse, marshalling a coalition of multiple enemies of the Sunnis could well deepen the local Sunni population's cooperation with ISIS. The air-only option has the opposite flaw. It would possibly hurt ISIS in Raqqah and other parts of the Sunni heartland, but with little means to stop ISIS from responding by expanding its area of control elsewhere.

The alternative strategies promise too much. They are vulnerable to failure and risk overcommitment of U.S. forces without reasonable prospects of major strategic benefits. Worse, if any of the proposals' intermediate steps fail to come to fruition, the United States will be left holding the bag, with no option other than committing more and more ground troops to a messier and messier conflict in Syria and Iraq.

FIGHT SMART

A plan to reclaim territory currently held by ISIS in Iraq that has more limited short-term objectives would be less vulnerable to failure. There is a fundamental strategic asymmetry between the situations in Syria and Iraq. In the short term—the next two years—Syria is likely to remain intractable. Whatever local ally works with the United States must fight a two-front war, confronting Syrian leader Bashar al-Assad and ISIS simultaneously—a task so daunting that it is hardly surprising that the Free Syrian Army has failed at it. In Iraq, by contrast, there are real possibilities for success. Indeed, success in Iraq can serve as a basis for achieving significantly more in Syria in the future.

Since early August, when the air campaign began, there have been over 1,200 U.S. air strikes against a variety of targets carried out by all manner of manned aircraft and drones. How do we know if the air campaign has been effective? Analysts and the administration have made conflicting claims. Here, more precision about the meaning of effectiveness is warranted.

There are two bases for assessing the effectiveness of air campaigns. The first is tactical: Have strikes succeeded in destroying ISIS fighters and materiel? The second is strategic: Have they contributed to thwarting ISIS' goals in the region?

Few disagree that air strikes have been effective at the tactical level. Coalition planes have destroyed countless ISIS vehicles, eliminated ISIS cadre, and disrupted oil-producing infrastructure. All the while, there have been no casualties on the Coalition side.

The lingering question, however, is whether tactical successes have amounted to a strategic one. It is at the level of strategic success that there has been the most ambiguity and confusion. Some critics argue that air power has failed to incapacitate and destroy ISIS, which is evidence, they say, that the United States needs a new strategy. However, the rapid elimination of ISIS is not a realistic objective for airpower, or any military campaign for that matter.

A more reasonable standard is whether airpower has been able to blunt ISIS' ability to take and hold territory. After all, ISIS has two overriding goals: expansion and consolidation of control. By this measure, the air campaign has achieved important success in blunting ISIS' offensive strategy of expanding its perimeter but has failed to counter ISIS' defensive strategy of consolidating Sunni-majority areas.

TACTICAL TRIUMPH

In June and July, ISIS achieved stunning victories when it overran important Sunni-majority areas, particularly Mosul, Iraq's second largest city. At this point, ISIS threatened to rapidly expand its areas of control into the Kurdish areas of northeastern Iraq and into the Shia areas in and around Baghdad as it moved toward Irbil, the Mosul Dam, Sinjar, and south of Baghdad. Given the recent loss of Mosul and the collapse of the Iraqi Security Forces in that city, there was reason to worry that, without international intervention, ISIS would win more territory.

The U.S. air campaign began in August and quickly halted ISIS' expansion beyond the Sunni majority areas. Air power was a valuable tool in limiting ISIS' potential expansion for three reasons. First, it could flexibly shift to the defense of various areas, depending on the degree of effort ISIS chose to exert against them. Second, U.S. airpower is especially effective at destroying clustered and massed enemy military units, and so limited the quantity of forces that ISIS could bring to bear in any one battle. Third, U.S. airpower could work in close conjunction with local ground forces, both bolstering their morale and serving as a force multiplier in specific ground encounters.

Put differently, the U.S. air campaign succeeded in blunting ISIS' drive toward Kurdish and Shia territory by using a strategy called "hammer and anvil." The strategy put ISIS in a catch-22: It could either choose to concentrate its forces to achieve local superiority over opposing ground troops and then be decimated by the United States' airpower "hammer"; or it could avoid airstrikes by dispersing its forces into small units and so be vulnerable to defeat by the opposing ground force "anvil." Either way, ISIS loses.

STRATEGIC STALEMATE

The current air campaign has failed, however, to prevent ISIS' consolidation of control over the Sunni areas in Iraq and Syria. Since mid-summer, ISIS has made territorial gains, most notably in Hit, Ramadi, Raqqah, and other areas deep inside the Sunni heartland.

In response, there have been airstrikes against ISIS' command-and-control structures and its revenue generating oil operations, strikes limited mainly by available intelligence. However, these strikes against leadership and economic targets have made little difference, and hitting them again would not change the situation.

Airstrikes against ISIS leaders and the group's economic base are unlikely to seriously weaken the group. To be sure, these "decapitation" tactics may, over time, kill leaders and destroy economically valuable assets—losses that could disrupt the group's operations. However, without additional measures to exploit this disruption when it occurs, the group can simply select new leaders and generate more resources, making the overall strategic impact of decapitation minimal. Since 2006, the United States has killed the past three leaders of ISIS and its forerunners, and each time, a new leader emerged with little trouble.

A new hammer-and-anvil approach—air power in combination with local ground forces—does offer a reasonable approach to rolling back ISIS control of Sunni areas, but current ideas that emphasize Kurdish or Shia-led Iraqi Security Forces would likely fail, if not make matters worse. As in Mosul and numerous other areas where ISIS has easily taken control, the Kurds and Shia are not willing to pay the costs to hold or retake Sunni-majority areas. Even if the United States could somehow coerce or cajole them into taking offensive action, that would likely to do more to further mobilize the 20 million Sunnis in the area to fight for ISIS. It would also take the option of a mutually acceptable settlement between Sunni and Shia leaders off the table. After all, ISIS is capitalizing on a widespread Sunni revolt in both Syria and Iraq to being governed (unfairly, as Sunni see it) by Shia-dominated governments in both places. Encouraging a return to greater Shia control is only going to deepen Sunni fears, strengthening rather than weakening ISIS.

HOW TO WIN

Defeating ISIS requires a new strategy for retaking Sunni territory. The strategy should incrementally build on the current hammer-and-anvil approach that has successfully blunted ISIS' expansion into Kurdish and Shia areas. The conditions are ripest for a Sunni anvil in Nineveh and Anbar provinces in Iraq, so these areas should be the focus of a new plan with four components.

The first objective should be to maintain the gains that the United States has already made. Accordingly, the United States should continue using airstrikes in Iraq and Syria to prevent ISIS from expanding territory under its control, especially at the expense of local allies. The air campaign has proved successful in halting ISIS' advances toward the Kurdish capital of Erbil and the Shia areas around Baghdad. The United States should deploy Special Forces and combat air controllers to support local allies, but only a very small number (fewer than 100) and only at the perimeter to minimize the risk of U.S. soldiers falling into ISIS' hands.

Second, the United States should secure a power-sharing agreement between the Iraqi government and Sunni tribes that allows greater autonomy for Sunni provinces—like that granted to the Iraqi Kurds. Oppression of the Sunnis by the Shia-dominated Iraqi government was a core reason mobilizing Sunni support for ISIS in the first place. Eliminating Sunni fears that a post-ISIS Iraq would simply replace domination by ISIS with a return to Shia domination will be key. In addition to political autonomy, Sunni control over the local police and security forces would be an important component of such a deal.

Third, the United States should expand the use of air power to limit ISIS' ability to move large forces freely between Syria and Iraq. Air power cannot completely seal the border: ISIS will still be able to move some forces across it. However, as the current air campaign has demonstrated, such tactics are highly effective against concentrated forces, and can stop ISIS from moving men and materiel in large concentrations, which significantly limits ISIS' ability to reinforce positions in Iraq (just as pressure on those positions mounts). This will provide a credible security guarantee to Iraqi Sunnis that ISIS' power over them is limited.

Fourth, it will be necessary to roll back ISIS in key Sunni areas. Together, the first three steps will weaken ISIS' control in Iraq. Guaranteeing Sunni political and security autonomy while containing ISIS expansion and mobility will make Sunnis more likely to resist ISIS. Meanwhile, strengthening local allies with minimal U.S. presence will not only improve the effectiveness of the air campaign but also empower the only force with a real incentive to roll back and defeat ISIS in combat. The strategy would strongly emulate the 2001 Afghan campaign, where local allies together with only 50 U.S. Special Forces managed to defeat the militarily superior and entrenched Afghan Taliban.

The crucial next step is to identify pockets of Sunni resistance to ISIS and support them. There are two obvious places to start. One is the Nineveh province police force, which numbered roughly 24,000 when ISIS took control of much of the province in June but was instantly cut off from all funds and weapons by the distrustful Shia-dominated government in Baghdad. The other is the Sunni tribes that have opposed ISIS in Anbar, such as the Jaghaifi, near Haditha, and Albu Nimr, near Hit, hundreds of whom were brutally killed by ISIS in an effort to suppress their opposition during the recent conquest. If supported by U.S. airpower and Special Forces, both groups have the self-interest and potential numbers to create the beginnings of a serious ground challenge to ISIS controlled territory in Anbar. Given that 1,500 U.S. Special Forces typically expect to train 15,000 local forces per year, even the current contingent of 3,000 advisers can expect significant results if focused on supporting a Sunni-based opposition force.

To maximize the prospects of successfully rolling back ISIS from Sunni areas in Iraq, the United States should resist getting drawn more deeply into Syria. For the next two years, the best way to weaken ISIS in Syria is indirectly. Specifically, reversing ISIS' momentum in Iraq will also likely weaken the group in Syria at least compared to other Sunni groups, changing its trajectory from a rising dominant force to one of numerous fragmented factions. As a result, pursuing this pragmatic plan is not only the best way to achieve real success against ISIS in Iraq; it is also the best approach to make Syria more manageable for the next administration.

The pragmatic plan to defeat ISIS is hardly perfect. It separates Syria from Iraq and so pushes off numerous important questions (such as Assad's political future and the fate of Raqqah, ISIS' putative capital). It requires brokering robust political and security autonomy for Sunnis that the Shia-dominated government in Baghdad would be loath to accept. However, by marshalling the United States' considerable strategic assets with local allies with a genuine interest in opposing ISIS control of territory, this plan has realistic prospects for meaningful and sustained success over the next two years.

ISIS Is Not a Terrorist Group

Why Counterterrorism Won't Stop the Latest Jihadist Threat

Audrey Kurth Cronin

After 9/11, many within the U.S. national security establishment worried that, following decades of preparation for confronting conventional enemies, Washington was unready for the challenge posed by an unconventional adversary such as al Qaeda. So over the next decade, the United States built an elaborate bureaucratic structure to fight the jihadist organization, adapting its military and its intelligence and law enforcement agencies to the tasks of counterterrorism and counterinsurgency.

Now, however, a different group, the Islamic State of Iraq and al-Sham (ISIS), which also calls itself the Islamic State, has supplanted al Qaeda as the jihadist threat of greatest concern. ISIS' ideology, rhetoric, and long-term goals are similar to al Qaeda's, and the two groups were once formally allied. So many observers assume that the current challenge is simply to refocus Washington's now-formidable counterterrorism apparatus on a new target.

But ISIS is not al Qaeda. It is not an outgrowth or a part of the older radical Islamist organization, nor does it represent the

AUDREY KURTH CRONIN is Distinguished Professor and Director of the International Security Program at George Mason University and the author of How Terrorism Ends: Understanding the Decline and Demise of Terrorist Campaigns. Follow her on Twitter @akcronin.

next phase in its evolution. Although al Qaeda remains dangerous—especially its affiliates in North Africa and Yemen—ISIS is its successor. ISIS represents the post–al Qaeda jihadist threat.

In a nationally televised speech last September explaining his plan to "degrade and ultimately destroy" ISIS, U.S. President Barack Obama drew a straight line between the group and al Qaeda and claimed that ISIS is "a terrorist organization, pure and simple." This was mistaken; ISIS hardly fits that description, and indeed, although it uses terrorism as a tactic, it is not really a terrorist organization at all. Terrorist networks, such as al Qaeda, generally have only dozens or hundreds of members, attack civilians, do not hold territory, and cannot directly confront military forces. ISIS, on the other hand, boasts some 30,000 fighters, holds territory in both Iraq and Syria, maintains extensive military capabilities, controls lines of communication, commands infrastructure, funds itself, and engages in sophisticated military operations. If ISIS is purely and simply anything, it is a pseudo-state led by a conventional army. And that is why the counterterrorism and counterinsurgency strategies that greatly diminished the threat from al Qaeda will not work against ISIS.

Washington has been slow to adapt its policies in Iraq and Syria to the true nature of the threat from ISIS. In Syria, U.S. counterterrorism has mostly prioritized the bombing of al Qaeda affiliates, which has given an edge to ISIS and has also provided the Assad regime with the opportunity to crush U.S.-allied moderate Syrian rebels. In Iraq, Washington continues to rely on a form of counterinsurgency, depending on the central government in Baghdad to regain its lost legitimacy, unite the country, and build indigenous forces to defeat ISIS. These approaches were developed to meet a different threat, and they have been overtaken by events. What's needed now is a strategy of "offensive containment": a combination of limited military tactics and a broad diplomatic strategy to halt ISIS' expansion, isolate the group, and degrade its capabilities.

DIFFERENT STROKES

The differences between al Qaeda and ISIS are partly rooted in their histories. Al Qaeda came into being in the aftermath of the 1979 Soviet invasion of Afghanistan. Its leaders' worldviews and strategic thinking were shaped by the ten-year war against Soviet occupation, when thousands of Muslim militants, including Osama bin Laden, converged on the country. As the organization coalesced, it took the form of a global network focused on carrying out spectacular attacks against Western or Western-allied targets, with the goal of rallying Muslims to join a global confrontation with secular powers near and far.

ISIS came into being thanks to the 2003 U.S. invasion of Iraq. In its earliest incarnation, it was just one of a number of Sunni extremist groups fighting U.S. forces and attacking Shiite civilians in an attempt to foment a sectarian civil war. At that time, it was called al Qaeda in Iraq (AQI), and its leader, Abu Musab al-Zarqawi, had pledged allegiance to bin Laden. Zarqawi was killed by a U.S. air strike in 2006, and soon after, AQI was nearly wiped out when Sunni tribes decided to partner with the Americans to confront the jihadists. But the defeat was temporary; AQI renewed itself inside U.S.-run prisons in Iraq, where insurgents and terrorist operatives connected and formed networks—and where the group's current chief and self-proclaimed caliph, Abu Bakr al-Baghdadi, first distinguished himself as a leader.

In 2011, as a revolt against the Assad regime in Syria expanded into a full-blown civil war, the group took advantage of the chaos, seizing territory in Syria's northeast, establishing a base of operations, and rebranding itself as ISIS. In Iraq, the group continued to capitalize on the weakness of the central state and to exploit the country's sectarian strife, which intensified after U.S. combat forces withdrew. With the Americans gone, Iraqi Prime Minister Nouri al-Maliki pursued a hard-line pro-Shiite agenda, further alienating Sunni Arabs throughout the country. ISIS now counts among its members Iraqi Sunni tribal leaders, former anti-U.S. insurgents, and even secular former Iraqi military officers who seek to regain the power and security they enjoyed during the Saddam Hussein era.

The group's territorial conquest in Iraq came as a shock. When ISIS captured Fallujah and Ramadi in January 2014, most analysts predicted that the U.S.-trained Iraqi security forces would contain the threat. But in June, amid mass desertions from the Iraqi army, ISIS moved toward Baghdad, capturing Mosul, Tikrit, al-Qaim, and numerous other Iraqi towns. By the end of the month, ISIS had renamed itself the Islamic State and had proclaimed the territory under its control to be a new caliphate. Meanwhile, according to U.S. intelligence estimates, some 15,000 foreign fighters from 80 countries flocked to the region to join ISIS, at the rate of around 1,000 per month. Although most of these recruits came from Muslim-majority countries, such as Tunisia and Saudi Arabia, some also hailed from Australia, China, Russia, and western European countries. ISIS has even managed to attract some American teenagers, boys and girls alike, from ordinary middle-class homes in Denver, Minneapolis, and the suburbs of Chicago.

As ISIS has grown, its goals and intentions have become clearer. Al Qaeda conceived of itself as the vanguard of a global insurgency mobilizing Muslim communities against secular rule. ISIS, in contrast, seeks to control territory and create a "pure" Sunni Islamist state governed by a brutal interpretation of sharia; to immediately obliterate the political borders of the Middle East that were created by Western powers in the twentieth century; and to position itself as the sole political, religious, and military authority over all of the world's Muslims.

NOT THE USUAL SUSPECTS

Since ISIS' origins and goals differ markedly from al Qaeda's, the two groups operate in completely different ways. That is why a U.S. counterterrorism strategy custom-made to fight al Qaeda does not fit the struggle against ISIS.

In the post-9/11 era, the United States has built up a trillion-dollar infrastructure of intelligence, law enforcement, and military operations aimed at al Qaeda and its affiliates. According to a 2010 investigation by *The Washington Post*, some 263 U.S. government organizations were created or reorganized in response to the 9/11 attacks, including the Department of Homeland Security, the National Counterterrorism Center, and the Transportation Security Administration. Each year, U.S. intelligence agencies produce some 50,000 reports on terrorism. Fifty-one U.S. federal organizations and military commands track the flow of money to and from terrorist networks. This structure has helped make terrorist attacks on U.S. soil exceedingly rare. In that sense, the system has worked. But it is not well suited for dealing with ISIS, which presents a different sort of challenge.

Consider first the tremendous U.S. military and intelligence campaign to capture or kill al Qaeda's core leadership through drone strikes and Special Forces raids. Some 75 percent of the leaders of the core al Qaeda group have been killed by raids and armed drones, a technology well suited to the task of going after targets hiding in rural areas, where the risk of accidentally killing civilians is lower.

Such tactics, however, don't hold much promise for combating ISIS. The group's fighters and leaders cluster in urban areas, where they are well integrated into civilian populations and usually surrounded by buildings, making drone strikes and raids much harder to carry out. And simply killing ISIS' leaders would not cripple the organization. They govern a functioning pseudo-state with a complex administrative structure. At the top of the military command is the emirate, which consists of Baghdadi and two deputies, both of whom formerly served as generals in the Saddam-era Iraqi army: Abu Ali al-Anbari, who controls ISIS' operations in Syria, and Abu Muslim al-Turkmani, who controls operations in Iraq. ISIS' civilian bureaucracy is supervised by 12 administrators who govern territories in Iraq and Syria, overseeing councils that handle matters such as finances, media, and religious affairs. Although it is hardly the model government depicted in ISIS' propaganda videos, this pseudo-state would carry on quite ably without Baghdadi or his closest lieutenants.

ISIS also poses a daunting challenge to traditional U.S. counterterrorism tactics that take aim at jihadist financing, propaganda, and recruitment. Cutting off al Qaeda's funding has been one of U.S. counterterrorism's most impressive success stories. Soon after the 9/11 attacks, the FBI and the CIA began to coordinate closely on financial intelligence, and they were soon joined by the Department of Defense. FBI agents embedded with U.S. military units during the 2003 invasion of Iraq and debriefed suspected terrorists detained at the U.S. facility at Guantánamo Bay, Cuba. In 2004, the U.S. Treasury Department established the Office of Terrorism and Financial Intelligence, which has cut deeply into al Qaeda's ability to profit from money laundering and receive funds under the cover of charitable giving. A global network for countering terrorist financing has also emerged, backed by the UN, the EU, and hundreds of cooperating governments. The result has been a serious squeeze on al Qaeda's financing; by 2011, the Treasury Department reported that al Qaeda was "struggling to secure steady financing to plan and execute terrorist attacks."

But such tools contribute little to the fight against ISIS, because ISIS does not need outside funding. Holding territory has allowed the group to build a self-sustaining financial model unthinkable for most terrorist groups. Beginning in 2012, ISIS gradually took over key oil assets in eastern Syria; it now controls an estimated 60 percent of the country's oil production capacity. Meanwhile, during its push into Iraq last summer, ISIS also seized seven oil-producing operations in that country. The group manages to sell some of this oil on the black market in Iraq and Syria—including, according to some reports, to the Assad regime itself. ISIS also smuggles oil out of Iraq and Syria into Jordan and Turkey, where it finds plenty of buyers happy to pay below-market prices for illicit crude. All told, ISIS' revenue from oil is estimated to be between $1 million and $3 million per day.

And oil is only one element in the group's financial portfolio. Last June, when ISIS seized control of the northern Iraqi city of Mosul, it looted the provincial central bank and other smaller banks and plundered antiquities to sell on the black market. It steals jew-elry, cars, machinery, and livestock from conquered residents. The group also controls major transportation arteries in western Iraq, allowing it to tax the movement of goods and charge tolls. It even earns revenue from cotton and wheat grown in Raqqa, the bread-basket of Syria.

Of course, like terrorist groups, ISIS also takes hostages, de-manding tens of millions of dollars in ransom payments. But more important to the group's finances is a wide-ranging extortion racket that targets owners and producers in ISIS territory, taxing every-thing from small family farms to large enterprises such as cell-phone service providers, water delivery companies, and electric utilities. The enterprise is so complex that the U.S. Treasury has declined to estimate ISIS' total assets and revenues, but ISIS is clearly a highly diversified enterprise whose wealth dwarfs that of any terrorist organization. And there is little evidence that Wash-ington has succeeded in reducing the group's coffers.

SEX AND THE SINGLE JIHADIST

Another aspect of U.S. counterterrorism that has worked well against al Qaeda is the effort to delegitimize the group by publiciz-ing its targeting errors and violent excesses—or by helping U.S. allies do so. Al Qaeda's attacks frequently kill Muslims, and the group's leaders are highly sensitive to the risk this poses to their image as the vanguard of a mass Muslim movement. Attacks in Morocco, Saudi Arabia, and Turkey in 2003; Spain in 2004; and Jordan and the United Kingdom in 2005 all resulted in Muslim casualties that outraged members of Islamic communities every-where and reduced support for al Qaeda across the Muslim world. The group has steadily lost popular support since around 2007; today, al Qaeda is widely reviled in the Muslim world. The Pew Research Center surveyed nearly 9,000 Muslims in 11 countries in 2013 and found a high median level of disapproval of al Qaeda: 57 percent. In many countries, the number was far higher: 96 per-cent of Muslims polled in Lebanon, 81 percent in Jordan,

73 percent in Turkey, and 69 percent in Egypt held an unfavorable view of al Qaeda.

ISIS, however, seems impervious to the risk of a backlash. In proclaiming himself the caliph, Baghdadi made a bold (if absurd) claim to religious authority. But ISIS' core message is about raw power and revenge, not legitimacy. Its brutality—videotaped beheadings, mass executions—is designed to intimidate foes and suppress dissent. Revulsion among Muslims at such cruelty might eventually undermine ISIS. But for the time being, Washington's focus on ISIS' savagery only helps the group augment its aura of strength.

For similar reasons, it has proved difficult for the United States and its partners to combat the recruitment efforts that have attracted so many young Muslims to ISIS' ranks. The core al Qaeda group attracted followers with religious arguments and a pseudo-scholarly message of altruism for the sake of the *ummah*, the global Muslim community. Bin Laden and his longtime second-in-command and successor, Ayman al-Zawahiri, carefully constructed an image of religious legitimacy and piety. In their propaganda videos, the men appeared as ascetic warriors, sitting on the ground in caves, studying in libraries, or taking refuge in remote camps. Although some of al Qaeda's affiliates have better recruiting pitches, the core group cast the establishment of a caliphate as a long-term, almost utopian goal: educating and mobilizing the *ummah* came first. In al Qaeda, there is no place for alcohol or women. In this sense, al Qaeda's image is deeply unsexy; indeed, for the young al Qaeda recruit, sex itself comes only after marriage—or martyrdom.

Even for the angriest young Muslim man, this might be a bit of a hard sell. Al Qaeda's leaders' attempts to depict themselves as moral—even moralistic—figures have limited their appeal. Successful deradicalization programs in places such as Indonesia and Singapore have zeroed in on the mismatch between what al Qaeda offers and what most young people are really interested in, encouraging militants to reintegrate into society, where their more prosaic hopes and desires might be fulfilled more readily.

ISIS, in contrast, offers a very different message for young men, and sometimes women. The group attracts followers yearning for not only religious righteousness but also adventure, personal power, and a sense of self and community. And, of course, some people just want to kill—and ISIS welcomes them, too. The group's brutal violence attracts attention, demonstrates dominance, and draws people to the action.

ISIS operates in urban settings and offers recruits immediate opportunities to fight. It advertises by distributing exhilarating podcasts produced by individual fighters on the frontlines. The group also procures sexual partners for its male recruits; some of these women volunteer for this role, but most of them are coerced or even enslaved. The group barely bothers to justify this behavior in religious terms; its sales pitch is conquest in all its forms, including the sexual kind. And it has already established a self-styled caliphate, with Baghdadi as the caliph, thus making present (if only in a limited way, for now) what al Qaeda generally held out as something more akin to a utopian future.

In short, ISIS offers short-term, primitive gratification. It does not radicalize people in ways that can be countered by appeals to logic. Teenagers are attracted to the group without even understanding what it is, and older fighters just want to be associated with ISIS' success. Compared with fighting al Qaeda's relatively austere message, Washington has found it much harder to counter ISIS' more visceral appeal, perhaps for a very simple reason: a desire for power, agency, and instant results also pervades American culture.

2015 ≠ 2006

Counterterrorism wasn't the only element of national security practice that Washington rediscovered and reinvigorated after 9/11; counterinsurgency also enjoyed a renaissance. As chaos erupted in Iraq in the aftermath of the U.S. invasion and occupation of 2003, the U.S. military grudgingly starting thinking about counterinsurgency, a subject that had fallen out of favor in the national security establishment after the Vietnam War. The most successful application of U.S. counterinsurgency doctrine was the 2007 "surge" in Iraq, overseen by General David Petraeus. In 2006, as violence peaked in Sunni-dominated Anbar Province, U.S. officials concluded that the United States was losing the war. In response, President George W. Bush decided to send an additional 20,000 U.S. troops to Iraq. General John Allen, then serving as deputy commander of the multinational forces in Anbar, cultivated relationships with local Sunni tribes and nurtured the so-called Sunni Awakening, in which some 40 Sunni tribes or subtribes essentially switched sides and decided to fight with the newly augmented U.S. forces against AQI. By the summer of 2008, the number of insurgent attacks had fallen by more than 80 percent.

Looking at the extent of ISIS' recent gains in Sunni areas of Iraq, which have undone much of the progress made in the surge, some have argued that Washington should respond with a second application of the Iraq war's counterinsurgency strategy. And the White House seems at least partly persuaded by this line of thinking: last year, Obama asked Allen to act as a special envoy for building an anti-ISIS coalition in the region. There is a certain logic to this approach, since ISIS draws support from many of the same insurgent groups that the surge and the Sunni Awakening neutralized—groups that have reemerged as threats thanks to the vacuum created by the withdrawal of U.S. forces in 2011 and Maliki's sectarian rule in Baghdad.

But vast differences exist between the situation today and the one that Washington faced in 2006, and the logic of U.S. counterinsurgency does not suit the struggle against ISIS. The United States cannot win the hearts and minds of Iraq's Sunni Arabs, because the Maliki government has already lost them. The Shiite-dominated Iraqi government has so badly undercut its own political legitimacy that it might be impossible to restore it. Moreover, the United States no longer occupies Iraq. Washington can send in more troops, but it cannot lend legitimacy to a government it no longer controls. ISIS is less an insurgent group fighting against an established government than one party in a conventional civil war between a breakaway territory and a weak central state.

DIVIDE AND CONQUER?

The United States has relied on counterinsurgency strategy not only to reverse Iraq's slide into state failure but also to serve as a model for how to combat the wider jihadist movement. Al Qaeda expanded by persuading Muslim militant groups all over the world to turn their more narrowly targeted nationalist campaigns into nodes in al Qaeda's global jihad—and, sometimes, to convert themselves into al Qaeda affiliates. But there was little commonality in the visions pursued by Chechen, Filipino, Indonesian, Kashmiri, Palestinian, and Uighur militants, all of whom bin Laden tried to draw into al Qaeda's tent, and al Qaeda often had trouble fully reconciling its own goals with the interests of its far-flung affiliates.

That created a vulnerability, and the United States and its allies sought to exploit it. Governments in Indonesia and the Philippines won dramatic victories against al Qaeda affiliates in their countries by combining counterterrorism operations with relationship building in local communities, instituting deradicalization programs, providing religious training in prisons, using rehabilitated former terrorist operatives as government spokespeople, and sometimes negotiating over local grievances.

Some observers have called for Washington to apply the same strategy to ISIS by attempting to expose the fault lines between the group's secular former Iraqi army officers, Sunni tribal leaders, and Sunni resistance fighters, on the one hand, and its veteran jihadists, on the other. But it's too late for that approach to work. ISIS is now led by well-trained, capable former Iraqi military leaders who know U.S. techniques and habits because Washington helped train them. And after routing Iraqi army units and taking their U.S.-supplied equipment, ISIS is now armed with American tanks, artillery, armored Humvees, and mine-resistant vehicles.

Perhaps ISIS' harsh religious fanaticism will eventually prove too much for their secular former Baathist allies. But for now, the

Saddam-era officers are far from reluctant warriors for ISIS: rather, they are leading the charge. In their hands, ISIS has developed a sophisticated light-infantry army, brandishing American weapons.

Of course, this opens up a third possible approach to ISIS, besides counterterrorism and counterinsurgency: a full-on conventional war against the group, waged with the goal of completely destroying it. Such a war would be folly. After experiencing more than a decade of continuous war, the American public simply would not support the long-term occupation and intense fighting that would be required to obliterate ISIS. The pursuit of a full-fledged military campaign would exhaust U.S. resources and offer little hope of obtaining the objective. Wars pursued at odds with political reality cannot be won.

CONTAINING THE THREAT

The sobering fact is that the United States has no good military options in its fight against ISIS. Neither counterterrorism, nor counterinsurgency, nor conventional warfare is likely to afford Washington a clear-cut victory against the group. For the time being, at least, the policy that best matches ends and means and that has the best chance of securing U.S. interests is one of offensive containment: combining a limited military campaign with a major diplomatic and economic effort to weaken ISIS and align the interests of the many countries that are threatened by the group's advance.

ISIS is not merely an American problem. The wars in Iraq and Syria involve not only regional players but also major global actors, such as Russia, Turkey, Iran, Saudi Arabia, and other Gulf states. Washington must stop behaving as if it can fix the region's problems with military force and instead resurrect its role as a diplomatic superpower.

Of course, U.S. military force would be an important part of an offensive containment policy. Air strikes can pin ISIS down, and cutting off its supply of technology, weapons, and ammunition by choking off smuggling routes would further weaken the group. Meanwhile, the United States should continue to advise and support the Iraqi military, assist regional forces such as the Kurdish Pesh Merga, and provide humanitarian assistance to civilians fleeing ISIS' territory. Washington should also expand its assistance to neighboring countries such as Jordan and Lebanon, which are struggling to contend with the massive flow of refugees from Syria. But putting more U.S. troops on the ground would be counterproductive, entangling the United States in an unwinnable war that could go on for decades. The United States cannot rebuild the Iraqi state or determine the outcome of the Syrian civil war. Frustrating as it might be to some, when it comes to military action, Washington should stick to a realistic course that recognizes the limitations of U.S. military force as a long-term solution.

The Obama administration's recently convened "summit on countering violent extremism"—which brought world leaders to Washington to discuss how to combat radical jihadism—was a valuable exercise. But although it highlighted the existing threat posed by al Qaeda's regional affiliates, it also reinforced the idea that ISIS is primarily a counterterrorism challenge. In fact, ISIS poses a much greater risk: it seeks to challenge the current international order, and, unlike the greatly diminished core al Qaeda organization, it is coming closer to actually achieving that goal. The United States cannot single-handedly defend the region and the world from an aggressive revisionist theocratic state—nor should it. The major powers must develop a common diplomatic, economic, and military approach to ensure that this pseudo-state is tightly contained and treated as a global pariah. The good news is that no government supports ISIS; the group has managed to make itself an enemy of every state in the region—and, indeed, the world. To exploit that fact, Washington should pursue a more aggressive, top-level diplomatic agenda with major powers and regional players, including Iran, Saudi Arabia, France, Germany, the United Kingdom, Russia, and even China, as well as Iraq's and Syria's neighbors, to design a unified response to ISIS.

That response must go beyond making a mutual commitment to prevent the radicalization and recruitment of would-be jihadists and beyond the regional military coalition that the United States has built. The major powers and regional players must agree to stiffen the international arms embargo currently imposed on ISIS, enact more vigorous sanctions against the group, conduct joint border patrols, provide more aid for displaced persons and refugees, and strengthen UN peacekeeping missions in countries that border Iraq and Syria. Although some of these tools overlap with counterterrorism, they should be put in the service of a strategy for fighting an enemy more akin to a state actor: ISIS is not a nuclear power, but the group represents a threat to international stability equivalent to that posed by North Korea. It should be treated no less seriously.

Given that political posturing over U.S. foreign policy will only intensify as the 2016 U.S. presidential election approaches, the White House would likely face numerous attacks on a containment approach that would satisfy neither the hawkish nor the anti-interventionist camp within the U.S. national security establishment. In the face of such criticism, the United States must stay committed to fighting ISIS over the long term in a manner that matches ends with means, calibrating and improving U.S. efforts to contain the group by moving past outmoded forms of counterterrorism and counterinsurgency while also resisting pressure to cross the threshold into full-fledged war. Over time, the successful containment of ISIS might open up better policy options. But for the foreseeable future, containment is the best policy that the United States can pursue.

ISIS on the Run

The Terrorist Group
Struggles to Hold On

Michael Pregent and Robin Simcox

The Islamic State of Iraq and al-Sham (ISIS) is starting to show some wear and tear. True, it pulled off the gruesome execution of Jordanian pilot Moaz al-Kasasbeh; true, it has attracted jihadists from across the world; and true, it still holds swaths of Iraq and Syria. But cracks are appearing in the self-styled Caliphate.

One reason is that, starting in the late summer, the U.S. intervention in Iraq helped stall the ISIS advance. Since then, troops have been able to go on the offensive and start expelling the terrorist group from the territory it holds; it has already lost Kobani, the north Syrian border town where much of the violence is centered, and has also suffered significant defeats in Bajyi, Jurf al-Sakhar, Diyala, and the Mosul Dam. In the grand scheme of things, this does not translate into much: Of the 55,000 square kilometres of territory ISIS controls, it has lost only 700—around one percent. But at least the momentum has been checked.

Now, a planned spring offensive, a joint U.S.-Iraqi effort to retake the Sunni capital of Mosul, could be a watershed moment. Iraqi Security Forces, Kurdish Peshmerga troops, and Sunni

MICHAEL PREGENT is Adjunct Lecturer at the College of International Security Affairs at National Defense University.

ROBIN SIMCOX is a Research Fellow at the Henry Jackson Society.

tribes—backed by U.S. air support and military advisers—will look to end ISIS' reign in the north and west Iraq, restoring government leadership in local towns and cities.

There are risks in this strategy. ISIS finds it easiest to take over Sunni areas where there is a looming threat of Shia or Pershmerga involvement. To retake Mosul, then, the coalition will have to avoid sending Peshmerga and Shia militias into the fray. The further these forces penetrate the Sunni enclave of Mosul, the likelier they are to push Sunnis into armed resistance.

Absent any Shia or Pershmerga threat to exploit, ISIS quickly loses tactical alliances, such as the Ansar al-Sunna, Army of the Men of the Naqshbandiyah Order (JRTN), and the 1920 Revolutionary Brigades. And when it fights alone, it loses. For example, ISIS had no allies to help it secure Kobani and the Mosul Dam. In both cases, a determined Iraqi ground force supported by U.S. weaponry and airstrikes defeated ISIS, a blow to its status as a formidable terrorist army.

These are not the only setbacks that ISIS has suffered recently. According to group spokespeople and media reports, there have been at least two different coup attempts against the ISIS leadership. Back in November, ISIS announced that it had thwarted a plot by a cell of Azerbaijanis who were plotting to kill ISIS members and encourage others to join an anti-ISIS faction. In recent days, details of a coup attempt against ISIS leadership in eastern Syria, led by Abu Ayyub al-Ansari, ISIS' governor in Raqqa, have emerged. Ansari and dozens of others were killed in response, and some of Ansari's fellow conspirators are thought to have fled Raqqa.

Furthermore, there seems to be a sense of growing disillusionment among recruits. The level of violence is extraordinarily high, even for a jihadist group. Outside the beheadings and burnings, prisoners are pushed off buildings, crucified, buried alive, and impaled. Female recruits are being coerced into ISIS sex camps and raped. According to one United Nations committee, the group is also torturing, crucifying, and burying children alive.

Meanwhile, foreign fighters, many of whom signed on to fight the Bashar al-Assad regime in Syria, have been pushed into conflict against other armed factions in Syria. Others are given menial tasks such as cleaning weapons and transporting dead bodies from the front line. Those who refuse their duties risk being labelled apostates and killed; and those who try to escape are equally likely to die. According to the Syrian Observatory for Human Rights, over 100 people who wished to leave the ISIS were executed between October and December 2014. This suggests that ISIS is increasingly turning on itself.

Something else that is slowing ISIS down: the group has been forced to govern the land that it currently holds. And it isn't going well. Wheat production has collapsed and electricity is sporadic. Hospital staff has fled and pharmaceutical supplies are in short supply. Water service was better under Assad and Iraq's former Prime Minister Nouri al-Maliki. ISIS may hold territory and enforce law and order, but it is clearly not governing.

Under these circumstances, the execution of Kasasbeh was a strategic error. It has—for now, at least—outraged Jordan. The last time the country suffered such a high-profile attack was in November 2005, when al Qaeda in Iraq killed 60 people in three coordinated attacks against hotels in Amman. This act not only cost the group a large amount of support across the region, it also led Jordan to ramp up its intelligence gathering. Within months, al Qaeda in Iraq's Jordanian leader, Abu Musab al-Zarqawi, was killed in a mission to which Jordanian intelligence had made a key contribution. If Jordan does the same this time, it will come at a time when ISIS can barely afford it.

On the other hand, the gains that Iraq and the West have made against ISIS are reversible if there is insufficient international will to press them home. It is critical that the United States stays engaged militarily. And partner nations, such as the United Kingdom, must increase support in order to share this burden.

It is also vital to recognize that, ultimately, only the Sunnis can clear their areas of ISIS' presence. One of the main reasons Iraqi security forces fled Mosul in June 2014 was that they had no political and economic ties there, and so were not interested in fighting and dying for it. The Sunnis are, provided that ISIS cannot convincingly argue that it is the sole protector against the Shia.

And that is why it is counterproductive for the United States to work alongside Iranian-backed militias against ISIS. The West cannot back Sunnis into a corner by offering them the choice of conflict with Shia militias—with the sectarian bloodletting that would surely follow—or an alliance with ISIS. A comprehensive U.S.-led strategy must involve partnering with Sunnis in fighting ISIS and reassuring Sunnis that there will be no Shia death squads after ISIS' defeat.

ISIS is on the run, but current U.S. policy isn't taking full advantage of that. Now is the time. If the West addresses deficiencies in its own strategy, weaknesses in ISIS' own framework will cause the group's downfall.

Ready for War With ISIS?

Foreign Affairs' Brain Trust Weighs In

W e at *Foreign Affairs* have recently published a **number of articles** on how the United States should respond to the Islamic State of Iraq and al-Sham. Those articles sparked a heated debate, so we decided to ask a broader pool of experts to state whether they agree or disagree with the following statement and to rate their confidence level about that answer.

The United States should significantly step up its military campaign against ISIS in Iraq and Syria.

Results

Full Responses

NAME	OPINION	CONFIDENCE LEVEL	COMMENT
OMAR AL-NIDAWI is an Iraqi commentator and political analyst.	Agree	10	The United States should double or triple the intensity of the air campaign. Airstrikes are producing effects that have allowed local forces to gain tactical advantage and win a number of engagements. That said, the number of strikes remains tiny compared to previous air campaigns in Iraq and Afghanistan. Furthermore, the airstrikes do not cover the whole theater; hence, reports of problematic Iranian airstrikes in Diyala in Iraq's east. More important than intensifying the military campaign, though, is developing a strategy for dealing with the Syrian situation. Without a solution for Syria, breaking ISIS in Iraq won't be sufficient.
RAAD ALKADIRI is Managing Director of IHS Energy. He was Assistant Private Secretary to the United Kingdom Special Representative to Iraq from 2003–04 and Political Adviser to the United Kingdom's Ambassador to Iraq from 2006 to 2007.	Disagree	8	
TONY BADRAN is a Research Fellow at the Foundation for Defense of Democracies.	Agree	6	An expansion of the campaign can only work if the United States abandons its current tacit alignment with Iran and its assets in the Levant and instead works with traditional U.S. allies in the region. There needs to be an integrated strategy that includes toppling the Assad regime and pushing back against the Iranian axis in the Levant.
AMATZIA BARAM is Professor Emeritus at the Department of the History of the Middle East and Director of the Centre for Iraq Studies at the University of Haifa, Israel.	Disagree	10	Under the present circumstances, there should be no additional U.S. involvement because the United States would appear to be an enemy of the Sunnis. However, once there is an agreement between Baghdad and the Sunni population, including the tribes of Anbar, Salah al-Din, and Nineveh, on a decentralized Iraq, the United States should help more in defeating ISIS.

HENRI J. BARKEY is a Professor of International Relations at Lehigh University. He served as a member of the U.S. State Department Policy Planning Staff, working primarily on issues related to the Middle East, the Eastern Mediterranean, and intelligence from 1998 to 2000.	Agree	8	I would distinguish between Syria and Iraq. I would prioritize Iraq, primarily because the United States has a certain responsibility there, but also because it has allies that it can presumably work with—Kurdish peshmerga and, to a slightly lesser extent, Iraqi security forces.
NORA BENSAHEL is Senior Fellow and Co-Director of the Responsible Defense Program at the Center for a New American Security.	Agree	3	U.S. President Barack Obama declared that the U.S. strategy is designed to "degrade and destroy" ISIS, but the current military operations are far more consistent with a strategy of containment—which may ultimately be the better strategic approach. The training and advising effort on the Iraqi side of the border needs to increase, but it's not yet clear how the United States would use force effectively on the Syrian side of the border.
RICHARD K. BETTS is Director of the Saltzman Institute of War and Peace Studies at Columbia University, an Adjunct Senior Fellow at the Council on Foreign Relations, and the author of American Force: Dangers, Delusions, and Dilemmas in National Security.	Disagree	3	There's little room to "step up" from air strikes and advisers, short of committing regular U.S. ground combat units, which is a Rubicon the United States should not cross. The little room that there is to increase the U.S. effort would involve extending U.S. advisers below brigade level and allowing them to accompany the Iraqi units they advise into combat.

STEPHEN BIDDLE is Professor of Political Science and International Affairs and Director of the Institute for Security and Conflict Studies at George Washington University. He is Adjunct Senior Fellow for Defense Policy at the Council on Foreign Relations.	Neutral	7	More force versus less force is the wrong way to think about this campaign. Someone else is going to be providing the bulk of the ground forces needed to defeat ISIS. But the likely providers (especially the Iraqi government) have serious corruption, cronyism, and sectarianism problems that will undermine the forces' effectiveness unless the United States can persuade their government to undertake painful reforms. U.S. airstrikes and contributions to the Iraqi Special Operations Forces are almost the only leverage Washington has to encourage these reforms. If it simply provides the forces without strings attached it will lose its only real leverage and actually make the situation worse: With a bigger U.S. safety net and no conditions, Baghdad has less need to swallow the castor oil of reform. Conversely, if the United States takes these forces off the table, it will also lose any prospective leverage. The only way to get anything like what the United States wants is to make conditional promises of major support—only if the government on the ground reforms—and provide this support in increments as the government reforms. So I would oppose "significantly stepping up the U.S. military campaign" unless this aid is used conditionally for leverage.
MAX BOOT is Jeane J. Kirkpatrick Senior Fellow for National Security Studies at the Council on Foreign Relations.	Strongly Agree	8	The current campaign against ISIS has little chance of success. The United States needs to expand its efforts, sending not only more aircraft and advisers, but also loosening the rules under which advisers operate. The United States must also do much more direct outreach to Sunnis in Iraq and Syria than is presently the case—and much more to counter Iranian machinations in both countries.

| RICK BRENNAN, Senior Political Scientist at the RAND Corporation, served as a Senior Adviser to the U.S. military in Iraq from 2006 to 2011. | Strongly Agree | 9 | The United States lacks a strategy to defeat ISIS in both Iraq and Syria. To date, the military campaign has been sufficient to contain ISIS, but it will be unable to defeat this terrorist organization without a significantly enhanced military mission. This doesn't mean that the United States should deploy conventional ground forces to fight in Iraq. However, what is needed are additional forces (boots on the ground) to conduct an enhanced advise-and-assist mission; force protection for U.S. facilities, diplomats, and service members; the employment of elite US counterterrorism forces to support Iraqi Special Operations Forces and target key ISIS leaders in Iraq and Syria; and the integration of U.S. Special Forces and tactical air control units into some of the Iraqi military organizations fighting ISIS—especially the peshmerga—to help build their capacity to conduct offensive operations to regain control of cities, towns, and villages that are now under the control of ISIS. This enhanced military campaign could require as many as 10,000–15,000 U.S. service members working in Iraq for at least three to five years. Failure to provide sufficient forces not only increases the risk of not achieving the goals and objectives established by Obama, but will likely result in U.S. forces having to remain in Iraq for a longer period of time. This military campaign must be a part of a broader political strategy that includes real progress in Iraq on issues associated with reconciliation and reintegration of minority groups that have been alienated by the Nouri al-Maliki government. The United States must use the crisis in Iraq to cause a fundamental political change within that country. In addition, the United States must develop a comprehensive strategy in the region that targets the causes of the Sunni-Shia civil war that now engulfs the Levant and serves as a breeding ground for violent extremist groups in Iraq, Syria, and the surrounding countries. |

MICHAEL BRÖNING is Executive Editor of Internationale Politik und Gesellschaft, a political magazine published by the Berlin-based Friedrich-Ebert-Stiftung.	Disagree	9	In the short run, the largest benefactor of a stepped-up military campaign against ISIS could well be ISIS. Instead of pursuing overly-ambitious objectives, the United States should let the "caliphate" provoke its own downfall. ISIS-propaganda aside, the threat needs to be put into perspective. What is needed is limited strikes in parallel to an economic and ideological quarantine of ISIS based on a broad coalition in the region. Instead of jeopardizing the development of such a coalition through all-out U.S. involvement, the United States should focus on bringing Iran in from the cold (before the current leadership is replaced by a more uncompromising generation of religious-nationalists).
DANIEL BYMAN is a Professor in the Security Studies Program at the Edmund A. Walsh School of Foreign Service at Georgetown University and a Senior Fellow at the Center for Middle East Policy at the Brookings Institution.	Agree	6	
ELIOT A. COHEN is Robert E. Osgood Professor at Johns Hopkins University's School of Advanced International Studies.	Neutral	5	I do not believe that going light is going to work, but I do not believe that this administration can competently devise, execute, and support a larger campaign. That is the core of the problem in recommending any policy to it at all.
BEN CONNABLE is a Senior International Policy Analyst at the RAND Corporation, a professor at the Pardee RAND Graduate School, and a retired Marine Corps intelligence and Arabic-speaking Foreign Area officer.	Neutral	10	No further increase in action should be made until the president and his staff outline a comprehensive strategy. The United States should only undertake military campaigns as part of a strategy with clearly defined end-state conditions, or at least definable national objectives.

MARTHA CRENSHAW is Senior Fellow at the Freeman Spogli Institute for International Studies and Professor, by courtesy, of Political Science at Stanford University.	Neutral	10	The answer depends on what type of military campaign, and in the service of what strategy.
RYAN CROCKER is Dean and Executive Professor at the George Bush School of Government & Public Service at Texas A&M University. He served as United States Ambassador to Iraq from 2007 to 2009 and United States Ambassador to Afghanistan from 2011 to 2012.	Strongly Agree	10	
AUDREY KURTH CRONIN is Distinguished Service Professor at George Mason University's School of Policy, Government, and International Affairs.	Disagree	10	The premise of the question is wrong. It frames the problem as a struggle between ISIS and the United States. Disaffected Iraqi Sunnis lead ISIS military efforts in Iraq—among them former Baathist military officers using U.S. weapons, trained by the United States. What would the United States be trying to do there? Defend a state whose inhabitants are attacking it? Plus, using U.S. military force in Syria aids the Assad regime. The United States should step up its military campaign to what end?
IVO H. DAALDER is President of the Chicago Council on Global Affairs. He was the U.S. Permanent Representative to NATO from May 2009 to July 2013.	Strongly Disagree	10	The United States needs to learn the lessons of Afghanistan and Iraq—its ability to affect significant internal change in other societies through the use of military force is extremely limited. Additional force isn't going to turn a failing strategy into a successful one.
JANINE DAVIDSON is Senior Fellow for Defense Policy at the Council on Foreign Relations.	Agree	6	Although there is probably a bit more that can be done militarily to stop ISIS' momentum and protect innocent civilians in Iraq and Syria, getting at the root causes of this conflict and creating lasting peace will take much more than military action by outside actors such as the United States.

ADEED DAWISHA is Distinguished Professor of Political Science at Miami University.	Disagree	8	The U.S. aerial campaign has scored some major successes. It has been instrumental in pushing ISIS fighters out of a number of strategic towns and areas in Iraq. It has relieved earlier pressure on Baghdad and Irbil. And it has inflicted damage on petroleum installations controlled by ISIS. Any stepping up will entail troops on the ground, and that will ignite opposition much wider than ISIS. Recent Friday sermons in Iraq (most notably by Muqtada al-Sadr) have echoed earlier calls to "confront the occupier!"
ERICA DE BRUIN is Assistant Professor of Government at Hamilton College.	Disagree	8	Without adequate ground troop support, even a stepped-up U.S. air campaign will not defeat ISIS. This is because defeating ISIS, like ending any other insurgency, requires sorting out insurgents from civilians. Local Sunni police forces in northern Iraq are likely best positioned to do so. Yet their efforts are being systematically undermined by a Shia-dominated central government that is fearful of putting too many weapons in the hands of Sunni forces. In the end, whether ISIS can be rolled back will depend less on the U.S. military campaign and more on the extent to which the Iraqi government can become more inclusive.
JAMES DOBBINS is Senior Fellow and Distinguished Chair in Diplomacy and Security at the RAND Corporation. He served as U.S. Ambassador to the European Union from 1991 to 1993, as Assistant Secretary of State for European Affairs in 2001, and as Special Representative for Afghanistan and Pakistan from May 2013 to July 2014.	Neutral	5	

PAULA DOBRIANSKY is Senior Fellow with the Future of Diplomacy Project at Harvard University's JFK Belfer Center for Science and International Affairs and Chair of the National Board of Directors of the World Affairs Councils of America. She served as Under Secretary of State for Democracy and Global Affairs from 2001 to 2009.	Strongly Agree	10	ISIS presents a major threat to U.S. national security interests. It is also vulnerable to a well-executed application of military force, coupled with an adroit diplomatic strategy with appropriate economic and ideological components. ISIS can be defeated with regional powers providing the primary capabilities on the ground.
MICHAEL SCOTT DORAN is a Senior Fellow at the Hudson Institute. He is a former Senior Director for the Middle East at the National Security Council and a former U.S. Deputy Assistant Secretary of Defense.	Strongly Agree	10	Allow me to use the analytic tools of American quantitative political science. In Iraq, our policy is, at best, containment— that is, half a policy. Meanwhile, in Syria, we have no policy at all—zero. As long as Syria remains a safe haven, ISIS wins. Zero times 0.5 equals zero. Now, multiply that total by the numerical coefficient of the fact that our actions in both Iraq and Syria strongly benefit Iran—by, in other words, a big fat zero. The little zero times the big fat zero equals the biggest zero of all.

| MICHAEL EISEN-STADT is Kahn Fellow and Director of The Washington Institute's Military and Security Studies Program. | Strongly Agree | 10 | Having vowed to "degrade, and eventually destroy" ISIS, Obama must demonstrate that momentum is shifting against ISIS and address the mismatch between means and ends in U.S. strategy. To do so, the United States needs to intensify air operations, commit special forces and combat controllers to guide air strikes, and further ramp up support for the Iraqi Security Forces, Kurdish peshmerga, and elements of the Syrian opposition. To do otherwise would be to further undermine U.S. credibility in the eyes of allies and adversaries, reduce U.S. leverage over coalition partners, create additional opportunities for Iran to expand its influence, and, most importantly, enable ISIS to attract additional recruits by allowing it to claim that it remains undefeated and unbowed. Intensified military activity is a necessary, but not sufficient, condition for success against ISIS, however. The biggest challenge is countering the jihadist ideology of ISIS and groups like it. The path that the United States and its Muslim partners have thus far taken—delegitimizing ISIS on religious grounds—by and large will not work for a coalition consisting of either "nonbelievers" or "apostate" regimes. Here, the key is to discredit ISIS by demonstrating that its caliphate project is doomed to fail and will bring only ruin to those who embrace it. Finally, ISIS and groups like it have demonstrated that they are highly resilient. Accordingly, the United States and its allies must husband their resources and prepare for a long struggle that may last for years to come. And the United States must avoid committing large numbers of ground forces to a military mission whose achievements—like those of other recent interventions in this part of the world—may well be ephemeral if efforts to counter jihadist ideology and to mobilize and organize opponents of ISIS fail. |

LEILA FAWAZ is the Issam M. Fares Professor of Lebanese and Eastern Mediterranean Studies at Tufts University.	Strongly Agree	6	
TANISHA FAZAL is Associate Professor of Political Science and Peace Studies at the University of Notre Dame.	Disagree	8	In Syria, increased strikes against ISIS would likely strengthen Syrian leader Bashar al-Assad's hand, especially given that the United States hasn't been willing or able to support the Free Syrian Army to the extent that it could take over the government. In Iraq, increased strikes could be more effective militarily and politically. But stepping up the military campaign would likely mean risking more American lives against an opponent that has shown itself to be fairly ruthless and capable. Even if such strikes were effective in the short term, I would be extremely skeptical about the results in the medium to longer term.
JAMES FEARON is Theodore and Frances Geballe Professor in the School of Humanities and Sciences and Professor of Political Science at Stanford University.	Strongly Disagree	8	First, the more we do, the less will be done by parties in the area who have more at stake and who (in some cases) the United States wants to build up their own capabilities. Second, although it is surely a horrible organization, ISIS does not pose that big a direct threat to the United States. Third, the more the United States does, the more it actually helps ISIS with the group's own storyline, which says that it is the most important and legitimate nationalist (in a way) opposition to foreign, infidel oppression exercised both directly and through corrupt local proxies. ISIS baited the United States to attack, and the United States took the bait. The more it does, the more it helps with ISIS' recruitment drives. Fourth, the only good way to get rid of ISIS in the long run is to let local actors deal with it and/or let the group fail at governing people who will quickly get sick of their rule.
PAGE FORTNA is Associate Professor in the Department of Political Science Saltzman Institute of War and Peace Studies at Columbia University	Disagree	5	

F. GREGORY GAUSE III is the John H. Lindsey '44 Chair, Professor of International Affairs, and Head of the International Affairs Department at the Bush School of Government and Public Service, Texas A&M University.	Disagree	8	The United States can hurt ISIS, but it cannot kill the group as a whole even with an expanded force, unless it stays there for a very long time. And that is not worth it.
FAWAZ A. GERGES is Professor of International Relations at the London School of Economics and Political Science and holder of the Emirates Professorship in Contemporary Middle East Studies.	Neutral	3	A bottom-up approach—working with local Sunni communities in Iraq and Syria by giving them a stake in the political and social system—is much more effective and less costly than U.S. military power.
SHADI HAMID is a fellow at the Brookings Institution's Center for Middle East Policy and author of *Temptations of Power: Islamists and Illiberal Democracy in a New Middle East*.	Strongly Agree	8	I would say the need to step up the U.S. military campaign against ISIS applies much more to Syria than Iraq, especially as it relates to supporting mainstream Syrian rebels against not just ISIS but the Assad regime as well
JOOST HILTERMANN is Chief Operating Officer of the International Crisis Group.	Strongly Disagree	10	There is no military solution to the challenges posed by ISIS. Any military campaign should therefore be accompanied by a concerted diplomatic effort to: lessen tension between Iran and Saudi Arabia, which is stoking the sectarianism in the region that is ISIS' best mobilizer; push the government in Baghdad to address local grievances through inclusive politics, the absence of which has led many Sunnis to believe that they have no defender other than ISIS; and bring about a negotiated political transition in Syria, where the regime has taken advantage of U.S. strikes to increase its attacks on remaining rebel-held areas—to ISIS' strategic advantage.

HEATHER HURL-BURT is Director of New Models of Policy Change at New America and Senior Fellow at Human Rights First.	Neutral	8	I would strongly support a plan that foresaw how a stepped-up U.S. military engagement could lead to a situation in Syria and in its neighbors that is more stable, more conducive to human freedom, and less conducive to extremist movements. Those are U.S. interests and values that would be worth asking our military to fight for. I have not yet seen anyone lay out such a strategy, however, and I'm not in favor of using force just to "do something."
JAMES JEFFREY is the Philip Solondz Distinguished Visiting Fellow at The Washington Institute. He was Deputy National Security Advisor from 2007–08 and U.S. Ambassador to Iraq from 2010 to 2012.	Strongly Agree	9	In fairness, the United States has done much—some of it to my surprise—since ISIS seized Mosul just six months ago, from stopping ISIS' expansion to putting together an international coalition and facilitating a new, more inclusive Iraqi government. The United States plans to further pressure ISIS. But given the sensible but hard goal of destroying ISIS, big questions remain: Whose boots should retake territory? What to do about Syria? Is time really on our side? The answer to the latter, I believe, is "No"; the United States thus needs to accelerate pressure on ISIS, put air controllers and/or advisors on the ground, and accommodate the Turks' Syrian no-fly/buffer zone idea.
ROBERT JERVIS is Adlai E. Stevenson Professor of International Affairs at Columbia University.	Disagree	4	
SETH JONES is Director of the International Security and Defense Policy Center at the RAND Corporation, as well as an Adjunct Professor at Johns Hopkins University's School for Advanced International Studies.	Agree	7	

ALI KHEDERY is Chairman and Chief Executive of the Dubai-based Dragoman Partners. From 2003 to 2009, he served as Special Assistant to five U.S. ambassadors and as a Senior Adviser to three heads of U.S. Central Command.	Neutral	10	The question misses the point in that no amount of bombing, covert action, or foreign assistance can make up for governments in Damascus and Baghdad that are seen as corrupt, murderous, unjust, or generally illegitimate in the eyes of millions of their citizens. ISIS and other jihadi groups are the manifestation of decades of bad governance, and so their ultimate defeat can only come from fundamentally good, inclusive governance. Vietnam, Afghanistan, Iraq, and now Libya should have taught us that bombs absent political strategies will only do harm.
LAWRENCE J. KORB is a Senior Fellow at the Center for American Progress. From 1981 to 1985, he served as U.S. Assistant Secretary of Defense.	Disagree	8	The struggle against ISIS will not be one waged militarily by the United States. The best that the United States can hope for militarily is to contain the group so that the countries in the region can have time to undermine the ISIS narrative.
ANDREW KREPIN-EVICH is President of the Center for Strategic and Budgetary Assessments.	Agree	9	
ELLEN LAIPSON is President and Chief Executive Officer of Stimson.	Strongly Disagree	8	

JOSHUA LANDIS is Associate Professor and Director of the Center for Middle East Studies at the University of Oklahoma. He is a member of the Department of International and Area Studies at the College of International Studies, and the President of the Syrian Studies Association.	Strongly Disagree	10	In Iraq, the United States supports the central state in its effort to retake ISIS-held territory. Because the state is weak, it is wise to contain and degrade ISIS until the Iraqi military can retake and hold ISIS-controlled towns. In Syria, the United States does not have a partner, but it claims to want to build up a vetted force to retake ISIS-held territory for minimal money. This is unlikely to happen. The Syrian state military is also weak and is being further weakened by sanctions and allied assistance to rebel militias. It is in no position to retake and hold most ISIS-held territory. Because the United States has no partner to occupy and govern the 35 percent of Syria that ISIS owns, it has no realistic option but to stick to its narrow policy of counterterrorism and trying to shove a weakened ISIS back into Syria. If Turkey were willing to send troops into Syria to help set up civil, non-Islamist rule in territory controlled by ISIS and al Qaeda, the United States could step up its campaign significantly and create a no-fly zone.
ROBERT J. LIEBER is Professor of Government and International Affairs at Georgetown University.	Agree	8	It's late. The situation is far worse than it might have been had the United States followed more robust policies earlier. As a result, the difficulties of a stepped-up military campaign have become significantly greater and the odds of success lower.

JANE HOLL LUTE is the President and Chief Executive Officer of the Council on CyberSecurity. She served as the Deputy Secretary of Homeland Security from 2009–13.	Disagree	8	War is a ground reality. Only an effective military response on the ground will set clear strategic limitations on what ISIS can achieve through violence. At this moment, the United States should not lead such a ground war. To send a clear message that ISIS cannot kill innocent Americans with impunity, however, the United States should hunt down those who do so. Yet, even against a brutally violent group such as ISIS, force cannot do all that needs doing—wars are known not just by what they destroy, but also by what they create. ISIS draws (mostly) young men from everywhere who will go anywhere because they feel like they belong nowhere. Against the backdrop of worldwide access to the Internet, where people can connect to ideas and each other instantly, and in the wake of the Arab Spring, which shattered the regional myth of an all-powerful centralized government, ISIS advances. Even if not on the ground, in the minds of those attracted to its message and (not incidentally) its means, ISIS advances. Force is legitimate to set clear limits to unacceptable behavior. But to solve the problem ISIS poses, we all must dig deeper for the enduring answer.
EDWARD N. LUTTWAK is Senior Associate at the Center for Strategic and International Studies.	Strongly Disagree	10	The Islamic State (ISIS itself is euphemistic) is actually the Sunni State. Its chief enemy is Iran, the United States' chief regional enemy.
MARC LYNCH is Director of the Institute for Middle East Studies and Professor of Political Science at the George Washington University.	Strongly Disagree	7	
KANAN MAKIYA is the Sylvia K. Hassenfeld Professor of Islamic and Middle Eastern Studies at Brandeis University.	Strongly Agree	10	

CARTER MALKA-SIAN is Principal Research Scientist in Strategic Studies at CNA. He is a former Political Officer for the U.S. State Department in Garmser, Afghanistan.	Neutral	4	As soon as possible, the United States should assist tribes already fighting ISIS with airstrikes, funds, and possibly special operations, but unless the government collapses, it should commit no conventional ground forces.
PETER R. MANSOOR, a retired Colonel in the U.S. Army, is Raymond E. Mason, Jr., Chair in Military History at the Ohio State University. He served as a Brigade Commander in Iraq in 2003–04 and as Executive Officer to General David Petraeus, Commander of the Multi-National Force-Iraq, in 2007–08.	Strongly Agree	10	ISIS is the face of evil in the modern world. Left unchecked, it would be highly destabilizing to the Middle East and a threat to the homeland and U.S. interests around the world. It must be confronted, degraded, and destroyed. The administration needs to formulate a coherent strategy to achieve this goal, resource it adequately, and prosecute it aggressively. Unfortunately, it is zero for three so far.
JOHN J. MEARSHEIMER is R. Wendell Harrison Distinguished Service Professor of Political Science at the University of Chicago.	Strongly Disagree	9	ISIS is not a serious threat to the core interests of the United States. Furthermore, there is no military strategy available to the United States that will solve the terrorism problem in the Middle East. Indeed, the more force the country uses, the worse the problem will get, as we have seen in recent years. The United States should rely on the local powers in the region to deal with ISIS.
BARAK MENDELSOHN is an Associate Professor of political science at Haverford College and a Research Fellow at Harvard Kennedy School's Belfer Center for Science and International Affairs.	Strongly Agree	9	Both strategic and moral imperatives require that the United States do more to rid the world of ISIS. Allowing ISIS to maintain an image of success and inevitability will make dislodging it, the ideology it presents, and methods it uses much more difficult. More robust action is also required to reestablish U.S. credibility and convince allies that it is serious.

MOHSEN MILANI is Professor of Politics and the Executive Director of the Center for Strategic and Diplomatic Studies at the University of South Florida.	Disagree	7	I disagree. Although U.S. airstrikes have stopped advances by ISIS, they alone will not defeat the group, even if they are significantly intensified. In Iraq, U.S. military intervention did not produce the desired outcome, and it resulted in unintended consequences. In fact, ISIS is a byproduct of the U.S. military occupation. It has now metastasized and is enmeshed in the mini cold war between Iran and Saudi Arabia and in Turkey's determination to reassert its regional role. At this time, when the Middle East is experiencing a tumultuous transformation, Washington must develop a regional strategy. The smart use of military force must be one component of this strategy, but cutting off the flow of money and weapons to terrorists in Syria and Iraq and undermining the ideological appeal of ISIS must be the other components. The strategy should also include rethinking of the U.S. approach toward Syria and Iran. The dilemma in Syria is that the organizations the West supports have been ineffective against Assad, whereas those the West does not trust, mainly ISIS and Al Nusra, have been effective. As for Iran, it has considerable experience fighting against ISIS and enjoys better relations with the Syrian and Iraqi governments than any other regional power. Iran has also helped the Kurdish peshmerga fight against ISIS. The United States and Iran share the common goal of defeating ISIS. Although there seems to have been an indirect coordination between Iran and the United States, as the recent airstrikes inside Iraq by Iranian Phantom jets indicate, much more bilateral collaboration is required in the future to defeat ISIS.
PAUL D. MILLER is a political scientist at the RAND Corporation. From 2007 to 2009, he was Director for Afghanistan and Pakistan on the U.S. National Security Council.	Agree	7	The campaign in Iraq and Syria is a Band-Aid. It is not a long-term solution. It is a necessary Band-Aid, but the United States still does not have a strategy for achieving stability and defeating jihadist groups in the Middle East (or South Asia).

JOHN MUELLER is a political scientist at Ohio State and a Senior Fellow at the Cato Institute.	Disagree	10	
CHANTAL DE JONGE OUDRAAT is Executive Director of SIPRI North America.	Disagree	9	
PAUL R. PILLAR is on the faculty of the Security Studies Program at Georgetown University. Concluding a long career in the Central Intelligence Agency, he served as National Intelligence Officer for the Near East and South Asia from 2000 to 2005.	Disagree	7	We should already have learned the lesson that application of external military force is not a substitute for internal political will that is necessary to end a civil war and the opportunities it provides for extremist groups.
KENNETH M. POLLACK is a Senior Fellow at the Brookings Institution and the author of Unthinkable: Iran, the Bomb, and American Strategy.	Agree	10	Although there is more that the United States could and should do in both Iraq and (especially) Syria, the real area where it needs to do a whole lot more is on the political side in both places.

BARRY R. POSEN is Ford International Professor of Political Science and Director of the Security Studies Program at the Massachusetts Institute of Technology.	Strongly Disagree	8	The only way to quickly step up U.S. participation would be to bomb more. I doubt that the current campaign is having an easy time finding good targets, and I fear that a more intense campaign would produce more collateral damage, which would produce more loyalty to ISIS and more new recruits. I fear that enhanced military advice, including providing advice in combat for Iraqi troops, would cause the troops to attack prematurely and that these attacks would not go well. The United States would then be seduced into adding more resources to avoid the loss of prestige that would come with the setback. I also fear that, even if these offensives could take back lost real estate, ISIS would revert to guerrilla warfare, which predominantly Shia and Kurdish troops would have a very difficult time suppressing. Again, pressure would rise for the United States to take a more direct role. In the latter two cases, a more direct role would not only increase direct costs to the United States but also validate the ISIS narrative. The group might be militarily weakened in a narrow sense but politically strengthened. The whole enterprise would be futile. Of course, this analysis is based on the facts as they have been presented. These facts might be false, in which case my analysis could be too pessimistic, or too optimistic.

ANDREW PARASIL-ITI is Director of the Center for Global Risk and Security at the RAND Corporation.	Neutral	8	U.S. military operations against ISIS should ideally complement diplomatic efforts toward a political settlement in Syria. There may be a role for more air strikes, intelligence coordination, and U.S. advisers in the fight against ISIS, but U.S. combat troops and no-fly/ safe zones would be high-risk options, especially in the absence of clarity about the U.S. endgame in Syria. On December 10, the U.S. Senate Foreign Relations Committee passed, by a vote of 10–8, a draft authorization for military force which does not authorize U.S. ground combat forces "except as necessary," meaning for protection and rescue and other non-combat actions. A CNN/ORC poll in late-November reports that 55 percent of Americans oppose U.S. ground forces in Iraq and Syria. The resolution also requires the Obama administration to provide a comprehensive strategy for Iraq and Syria. This strategy should be a prerequisite to any discussion of U.S. military escalation. The draft authoriza-tion calls for the United States "to the greatest extent possible act in concert or cooperation with the security forces of other countries in the region to counter the grave threat to regional stability and international security posed by [ISIS]." Here, the United States could benefit from stepped up efforts by Turkey and other U.S. allies to disrupt ISIS' financial, trade, transit, and supply networks and from the shared interest of Iran in battling ISIS.
CARLA ANNE ROBBINS is Adjunct Senior Fellow at the Council on Foreign Relations and Clinical Professor of National Security Studies at Baruch College's School of Public Affairs.	Disagree	8	

LINDA ROBINSON is Senior International Policy Analyst at the RAND Corporation.	Agree	8	The United States needs a more robust advisory and assistance mission, strategic patience, and political conditions on the Iraqi government in order to have a good chance of succeeding. Key allies and Syrians will not fight unless a post-Assad succession is part of the plan. Diplomatic expertise and a political strategy is needed to guide this effort.
BASSEL F. SAL-LOUKH is Associate Dean of the School of Arts and Sciences and Associate Professor of Political Science at the Lebanese American University.	Strongly Agree	10	The specter of ISIS haunting Iraq and Syria and the rest of the region is part of the blow-back from the 2003 U.S. invasion and occupation of Iraq and, later, the sectarianization of the grand geopolitical contest between Saudi Arabia and Iran triggered by this invasion. Although this contest predates the Arab uprisings, its sectarianization peaked on the morrow of the Arab Spring. It is increasingly clear that the regimes that played an instrumental role in the formation of the Frankenstein that is ISIS are unable to contain it anymore. Consequently, regional stability, to say nothing of domestic peace, require a much more robust U.S. military effort against ISIS, one that entails close coordination not only with America's regional allies, but its opponents as well.
JEREMY SHAPIRO is a Fellow with the Project on International Order and Strategy and at the Center on the United States and Europe at the Brookings Institution and a former member of the U.S. State Department's Policy Planning Staff.	Disagree	6	ISIS is a symptom of the disorder and dysfunction in the Middle East. And although destroying ISIS with massive U.S. military power might satisfy the United States' sense of justice and desire for revenge, it will not address the underlying cause of instability in the region that gave rise to ISIS. As the United States has learned to its own cost, that will require a local and regional political effort that no amount of U.S. military power can provide. The country can continue to send young Americans to destroy U.S. enemies in Iraq and Syria for many generations, but that will never buy the peace it seeks. While working to contain the ISIS threat, the United States needs to encourage local efforts, and part of that involves demonstrating to local actors that the U.S. military will not serve as their air force or crush their enemies.

ROBIN SIMCOX is a Research Fellow at the Henry Jackson Society.	Strongly Agree	9	ISIS relies on safe havens in both Iraq and Syria to thrive, but not enough is being done in either theater to defeat the group. In Syria, expanding the effort to arm non-jihadist rebels is required, as is a no-fly zone to protect them from Assad. In Iraq, the West must restore Sunni tribes' trust in its commitment to Iraq and help them build the capacity to retake their lost territory. Yet to be truly effective, boots on the ground to accompany Iraqi partners will also be required.
STEVEN SIMON is Senior Fellow at the Middle East Institute in Washington, D.C.	Disagree	5	It's not obvious what "significantly step up" means. Small special forces have already been inserted into Syria for the purposes of hostage rescue and, in Iraq, there will soon be a couple thousand advisors. The United States is flying hundreds of sorties against ISIS. These operations will increase in intensity as more intelligence is built up—an alluvial process that takes time. All this seems to add up to something significant already. The issue is how much is enough to keep the government in Baghdad more or less secure from disabling ISIS attacks. The currently projected level of effort should accomplish this goal, recognizing that Iraqi forces will remain weak for a long time. The ISIS threat to the U.S. homeland does not warrant more intensive involvement at this point—it's mainly an intelligence and law enforcement problem.
ANNE-MARIE SLAUGHTER is President and CEO of New America and Bert G. Kerstetter '66 University Professor Emerita of Politics and International Affairs at Princeton University. From 2009 to 2011, she served as Director of Policy Planning for the United States Department of State,	Neutral	10	The United States' campaign against ISIS has no chance of being successful over the long term unless the country is willing to take direct action against the Syrian regime at the same time.

PETER SLUGLETT is Director of the Middle East Institute of the National University of Singapore.	Strongly Agree	8	Of course, the rise of ISIS is partly a consequence of failed U.S. policies in Iraq, but the fact is that only a robust response from the United States now is likely to make a significant dent in ISIS' progress. I wish this were not the case, but I see no other immediate solution.
JESSICA STERN is a Fellow at the FXB Center for Health and Human Rights at the Harvard School of Public Health and a Lecturer in Government at Harvard University.	Disagree	5	
ANDREW J. TABLER is senior fellow at the Washington Institute for Near East Policy.	Neutral	8	Washington needs to wield much more political power if it seeks to "defeat" or "destroy" ISIS. U.S. airstrikes may be "degrading" jihadists in Iraq and Syria, but the Obama administration's uncoordinated and slow roll-out of a program to train and equip Syria's moderate rebels has, thus far, strengthened the cause of jihadists in Syria and Iraq. When the United States began striking ISIS and al Qaeda groups in Syria, the latter turned against Western-backed moderate rebels that Washington plans to arm to take on ISIS. Washington's unwillingness to forge political agreement with its Sunni allies concerning efforts against the Iranian-backed and Assad-dominated rump state in Syria means that Washington is unlikely to have sufficient buy-in from Syria and Iraq's neighbors to seal their borders and help train forces that can enter the Sunni-dominated areas of eastern Syria and western Iraq and root out ISIS. Washington's negotiations with the Islamic Republic of Iran over its nuclear program, combined with a recent letter from Obama to Iran's Supreme Leader pledging cooperation against ISIS following a nuclear deal, has only exacerbated suspicions among Sunni allies that Washington's ISIS strategy will primarily benefit Iran. Without getting the Sunnis politically and militarily on board in Syria, Iraq, and the rest of the region, defeating or destroying ISIS will remain an elusive goal.

SHIBLEY TELHAMI is the Anwar Sadat Professor for Peace and Development at the University of Maryland, College Park, and Non-Resident Senior Fellow at the Brookings Institution.	Strongly Disagree	9	The United States should limit action to airpower and focus principally on Iraq, with preventive planning in Jordan. Ground forces could become part of problem, not solution, especially in Syria. It is not enough to stop ISIS' progress militarily; the United States must plan for the morning after it stops its operations. Ask: Will ISIS or a replacement re-emerge soon after U.S. attacks stop? Many Arabs do fear ISIS and dislike its agenda, but some also dislike existing Arab regimes even more, and ISIS is stepping into that vacuum. One source of the problem cannot itself become part of the solution.
STEPHEN M. WALT is the Robert and Renee Belfer Professor of International Affairs.	Strongly Disagree	8	
BARBARA F. WALTER is a Professor of International Relations and Pacific Studies and Affiliated Faculty of Political Science at UC San Diego.	Strongly Disagree	9	We have absolutely no evidence that military attacks against ISIS will shorten these wars. In fact, if anything, historical evidence suggests that it will lengthen them. We also have no evidence that military attacks against ISIS will deliver a stable government in either Iraq or Syria that serves in the best interests of a majority of Iraqi or Syrian citizens (or the best interests of the United States). Given these uncertainties, less intervention is advised, not more.
PAUL WOLFOWITZ is a visiting scholar at the American Enterprise Institute. He is former President of the World Bank, U.S. Ambassador to Indonesia, U.S. Deputy Secretary of Defense, and Dean of the Paul H. Nitze School of Advanced International Studies at Johns Hopkins University.	Agree	9	Curiously, for an administration that asserts so often that there can't be purely military solutions to problems, its approach to this one seems to be purely military. The United States also needs a political strategy to separate Iraqi Sunnis from ISIS, to separate Baghdad from Tehran and bring it closer to the Sunni Arabs, and to separate Assad's "outer circle" from the hard core supporters. All of this would be facilitated by a stronger military campaign against Assad as well as ISIS, which would convince the people the United States needs to influence that the United States is going to be a decisive factor in defeating ISIS.

13324230R00097

Printed in Great Britain
by Amazon.co.uk, Ltd.,
Marston Gate.